Samuel Beckett

D1425451

Titles in the series Critical Lives present the work of leading cultural figures of the modern period. Each book explores the life of the artist, writer, philosopher or architect in question and relates it to their major works.

In the same series

Jean Genet
Stephen Barber

Michel Foucault
David Macey

Pablo Picasso
Mary Ann Caws

Franz Kafka
Sander L. Gilman

Guy Debord
Andy Merrifield

Marcel Duchamp
Caroline Cros

James Joyce
Andrew Gibson

Frank Lloyd Wright
Robert McCarter

Jean-Paul Sartre
Andrew Leak

Noam Chomsky
Wolfgang B. Sperlich

Jorge Luis Borges
Jason Wilson

Erik Satie
Mary E. Davis

Georges Bataille
Stuart Kendall

Ludwig Wittgenstein
Edward Kanterian

Octavio Paz
Nick Caistor

Walter Benjamin
Esther Leslie

Charles Baudelaire
Rosemary Lloyd

Jean Cocteau
James S. Williams

Sergei Eisenstein
Mike O'Mahony

Salvador Dalí
Mary Ann Caws

Simone de Beauvoir
Ursula Tidd

Edgar Allan Poe
Kevin J. Hayes

Gertrude Stein
Lucy Daniel

Pablo Neruda
Dominic Moran

Samuel Beckett

Andrew Gibson

REAKTION BOOKS

To the Kiberds

Published by Reaktion Books Ltd
33 Great Sutton Street
London EC1V 0DX, UK

www.reaktionbooks.co.uk

First published 2010

Printed and bound in Great Britain
by CPI Antony Rowe, Chippenham, Wiltshire

British Library Cataloguing in Publication Data
Gibson, Andrew, 1949–
    Samuel Beckett. – (Critical lives)
    1. Beckett, Samuel, 1906–1989.
    2. Dramatists, Irish – 20th-century – Biography.
    I. Title   II. Series
    822.9'12-DC22

ISBN: 978 1 86189 517 2

Contents

Nor can there be work so great
As that which cleans man's dirty slate.
W. B. Yeats

Abbreviations

WORKS

CDW	*Complete Dramatic Works*
CP	*Collected Poems*
CSP	*Complete Shorter Prose 1929–1989*
DFMW	*Dream of Fair to Middling Women*
DI	*Disjecta*
EAG	*En attendant Godot*
GD	*German Diaries*
ISIS	*Ill Seen Ill Said*
MPTK	*More Pricks than Kicks*
MU	*Murphy*
TR	*Trilogy: Molloy, Malone Dies, The Unnamable*
WH	*Worstward Ho*

Except where indicated, all translations of secondary literature in French and German are my own, as are translations from the French texts in *Disjecta*.

Introduction: Fuck Life

In one of Beckett's late plays, we encounter a haunting figure.
A prematurely old woman with famished eyes sits rocking in a
rocking-chair. A voice speaks, telling her the story of a woman
whose vain hope of human contact led her to the rocking-chair
in which her mother 'sat and rocked . . . till her end came' (*CDW*,
p. 440). There she sat down and rocked herself,

> saying to the rocker
> rock her off
> stop her eyes
> fuck life
> stop her eyes
> rock her off
> rock her off (*CDW*, p. 442)

The play ends with these lines.

'Fuck life' is not a sentiment ever likely to win assent from
biographers. Obviously and by definition, biography can hardly
accommodate it. Biography is necessarily affirmative. The assumption that life has value, that individual lives deserve monuments,
substantial and often bulky tributes, is intrinsic to the genre.
Furthermore, the life that has value is specific in kind. It is life
as it has already been lived, life as grasped in retrospect. That
the subject of the biography might for instance be a writer who

'Fuck life': Siân Phillips in *Rockaby* at the Barbican Pit, London, 2006.

conceives of his or her art as a criticism of life, as a mode of speculation, an enquiry into prospects not retrospects, makes no difference to biographical discourse. It is presumably better to have biographies of, say, Swift, Blake, Rimbaud, Artaud and Woolf than not to have them. Yet one might argue all the same that, however close or sympathetic their biographers to these writers, biography necessarily sets its face against the most urgent admonitions of their art. In this respect, modern biography might even seem to have repeatedly collided with modern art, stoutly resisting its implications.

This has been precisely the case with Samuel Beckett. The biographies proceed in the opposite direction to his writings. For reasons that still puzzle us, Beckett's art repeatedly turns towards *minima*. James Knowlson's widely and rightly lauded, authorized, vast and fact-crammed life amounts to 872 pages. At 646 pages, Anthony Cronin's competitor volume is hardly much more modest. On the one hand, Knowlson and Cronin's biographies are essential reading. Indeed, they complement each other, Cronin's grasp of the Irish Beckett and his imaginative feeling for the miserable extravagance of his subject leavening Knowlson's awesome meticulousness, his exemplary scholarly care. I am humbly indebted to both throughout this short account. On the other hand, it seems to me to be well worth trying to write something more like a minimalist life of Beckett, by way of closing the gap between the biographical project and his own. What does Beckett's life look like if narrated in more Beckettian terms?

Beckett wrote of humanism that it was 'a word that one reserves for the times of the great massacres' (*DI*, p. 131). He repeatedly stripped his characters of the attributes held most to distinguish man as lord of creation. His works resound with indictments of humanist self-aggrandizement. He sees humanism as rooted in a will to be pleased with oneself. His jibes at its expense range from the scathing to the comic to the more or less mildly ironical. 'It's human,' says the Unnamable, 'a lobster couldn't do it' (*TR*, p. 375). Yet, at the same time, he never seriously lapses into the brutal repudiation of common humanity that so marred the work of certain contemporaries, like Céline (whose novels Beckett much admired). He merely understood very well that humanism has little to do with human beings. So what happens if one forsakes the familiar humanist conspectus and tries to write a biography of Beckett without automatically and everywhere placing the self-evidently treasurable, unique human being at its centre? What happens if we conceive of Beckett as, rather like Giorgio Agamben, re-imagining 'the human thing'? I hope to provide at least one possible answer to these questions in what follows.

The value of Beckettian minimalism obviously raises certain questions for his biographers. But so too does the nay-saying drive with which I began, and from which it is inextricable. Fuck life:

> MRS ROONEY: It is suicide to be abroad. But what is it to be at home, Mr Tyler, what is it to be at home? A lingering dissolution . . . I beg your pardon?
> MR TYLER: Nothing, Mrs Rooney, nothing, I was merely cursing, under my breath, God and man, under my breath, and the wet Saturday afternoon of my conception. (*CDW*, p. 175)

Beckett's characters curse a great deal. They excoriate the 'shitball' or 'old muckball' on which they find they have no alternative but to live. They have little or no time for 'the execrable frippery known as the non-self and even the world' (*CDW*, p. 222, *CSP*, pp. 31–2). 'Christ what a planet' (*CDW*, p. 183): here life is an 'endless winter year after year' (*CDW*, p. 393), and 'the whole ghastly business looks like what it is, senseless, speechless, issueless misery' (*TR*, p. 13). In *Endgame*, Hamm describes a madman

> who thought the end of the world had come. He was a painter – and engraver. I had a great fondness for him. I used to go and see him, in the asylum. I'd take him by the hand and drag him to the window. Look! There! All that rising corn! And there! Look! The sails of the herring fleet! All that loveliness! [*Pause.*] He'd snatch away his hand and go back into his corner. Appalled. All he had seen was ashes. (*CDW*, p. 113)

Beckett does not offer charming pictures of herring fleets. Recent commentators on Beckett have sought to emphasize rather less gloom-inducing and more contemporary aspects of his work, like technology and the body. Yet for all the quality of much of the commentary, it is hard to deny that Beckett's true interest is in the madman's ashes, or what Walter Benjamin described as the pile of our debris that grows constantly skyward.[1]

But there is even more trouble in store for the biographer. Beckett's characters are not only unenthusiastic about life. They are also dismissive of life-writing. This is peculiarly evident in the four *Stories*. They tell us that, properly speaking, life is an 'inenarrable contraption' (*TR*, p. 115). To write autobiography is to write something other than one's history:

> I have always spoken, no doubt always shall, of things that never existed, or that existed if you insist, no doubt always will, but not with the existence I ascribe to them. (*CSP*, p. 35)

When it comes to telling stories, the narrators of the *Stories* run up against rudimentary obstacles that ought to be enough to unnerve the jauntiest and most self-confident of biographers. The simplest representational tasks are fraught with difficulty: 'But the faces of the living, all grimace and flush,' says one narrator, 'can they be described as objects?' (*CSP*, p. 38). The shape one gives a life seems arbitrary ('nonsuch perhaps, who cares', *CSP*, p. 60). 'I don't know why I told this story', says the narrator of 'The Expelled', 'I might just as well have told another' (*CSP*, p. 63). How could a biography that took this sentence as its epigraph conceivably go on? As the narrator of 'The Calmative' makes ironically clear, the true function of life-writing is not to give us life but to screen us from it, to act as a calmative or tranquillizer, to provide us with the illusion of having bearings where there are none. One particular Beckettian figure suggests that life-stories should consist of facts and be efficiently recounted. But they should also be 'positively fairy-like in places'. This clears the ground so that we may turn our attention to more important matters, 'thighs . . . arses, cunts and environs' (*CSP*, pp. 72–73).

Beckett seems to have set little or no store by biography as a serious mode of knowledge. Drink, sex, games, social life, daily routines: little is to be gleaned from such pedestrian themes. They are the means by which the biographer presumes to extract 'the picture of the artist's individuality' whilst in fact reducing it to a 'cartoon' (*DI*, p. 61).[2] But Beckett also clearly accepted that biographies get written. The effort to resist capture in a modern biography was bound to prove singularly futile. Thus when, in 1971, Deirdre Bair asked him for permission to write his life, he responded with generous indifference. He would, he said, neither help nor hinder her. At the same time, he knew it would be as well to authorize a biography by a trustworthy scholar with an established reputation. So when the self-dubbed 'fledgling biographer' Knowlson approached him again in 1989, the year of his death, even whilst insisting that 'his life was separate from his art',[3] Beckett agreed to his request. More specifically, as Knowlson himself candidly informs us, his subject replied with a single sentence: 'To biography of me by you it's Yes'.[4] This recalls his response when asked for his view of the Spanish Civil War: 'ɪUPTHEREPUBLIC!'.[5] He had a habit of twisting formal phrases out of true, as though part of him were rebelling against the very terms to which he was consenting. Whilst not an indication of recalcitrance, his message to Knowlson serves as a modest injunction: do not look for me in the usual places, for I shall not be found there.

How, then, might one re-imagine the life of a writer apparently so sceptical of the truth-content of biography, in terms respectful of that scepticism? Still more problematically: how might one re-imagine the biography of a man who so often appears to loathe the *bios*? How does one write a fuck-life? How does one write a fuck-life of a writer whose works (and characters) repeatedly appear to say 'Fuck life-writing'? From 1928 to 1930, in somewhat desultory fashion, Beckett taught at what has been one of the great educational institutions in history, the École Normale Supérieure in Paris. The École Normale's conception of intellectual life for much of the twentieth century has no parallel in the contemporary Anglo-American world, and is almost incomprehensible to it. That is why English and American intellectuals have been so awed by its alumni. Though he was not an alumnus himself, *normaliens* have repeatedly thought of Beckett as one of themselves. Like many others, they have also thought of him as an imaginative writer unusually close to the traditions of continental European philosophy, of which, in the twentieth century, the École Normale was probably the most significant crucible.

Not that the virtues of *normaliens* were always unrelieved. One of Beckett's contemporaries, Robert Brasillach, was executed as a Nazi collaborator. Another, a friend of Beckett's, Georges Pelorson, became a prominent figure in the Vichy regime. But what I want to stress here is the *normaliens'* habit of writing lives that are non-lives. Sartre's memoir of Merleau-Ponty scarcely mentions a single fact of the kind that we would usually associate with a life. Canguilhem's life of Cavaillès mentions facts only where they seem part of a life conceived of as a project of thought.[6] Given what I shall say later of the importance of the ambience of the École Normale Supérieure for understanding Beckett, these might seem to be the obvious models to follow. But there is at least one patent difficulty with this line of argument. How does one write an intellectual biography of Beckett without simply producing yet another critical monograph, a chronological and consecutive reading of his works? There are many of these already. I've written one myself.[7]

Faced with this dilemma, I have chosen a slightly different expedient, which I hope offers its own kind of illumination (or *chiaroscuro*), but which also corresponds to my own particular understanding of Beckett's project. In 'First Love', the narrator succinctly declares that 'it's always the same sky and never the same sky' (*CSP*, p. 38). This seems to me to express a paradox that is central to Beckett's art. As the narrator of 'The End' suggests, the universal muck is not 'embodied in' particular muck. It is never known otherwise than in and as mucky particularities. This means that it is never fixed and final. At the very least, there is always the possibility of adding to it, as the same narrator says when he speaks of a 'little kingdom' contrivable in its midst (a kingdom to which there would be a further mucky addition, in that he also speaks of shitting on it, *csp*, p. 98). In *Krapp's Last Tape*, Krapp speaks of

> separating the grain from the husks. . . . The grain, now what I wonder do I mean by that. I mean . . . [*hesitates*] . . . I suppose I mean those things worth having when all the dust – when all *my* dust has settled. (*cdw*, p. 217)

Krapp's self-correction, his shift from generality to his own particular condition, insists on the specificity of difficulty, suffering and waste. This shift is not untypical of Beckett's characters. Again and again, the 'life' with which they struggle or against which they set their face turns out to be, not a universal expressed in a particular form, but a particular form taken for a universal one.

In other words, there is no universal *bios* to loathe. As Foucault above all instructed us, the *bios* is always historical. There have been many life-haters. But since they have known life only in and as particular historical occasions, they have always hated particular historical versions of life, even when they have asserted the opposite. There are times when the compulsion to stare at Benjamin's growing pile of debris is well-nigh unmasterable. There are others when it can seem negligible. Beckett produced his *œuvre* within historical cultures quite different to ours. That is why we goggle at him with such exceptional fascination.

What I want to do here, with such dismal vividness as I can muster, is write an intellectual life of Beckett, but also to situate it in relation to a succession of discrete contexts. The contexts will historicize and perhaps in some degree explain the desire to have done with life, to 'Throw up for good. Go for good. . . . Good and all' (*wh*, p. 8), however lacking in finality or ironically couched that desire may be. On the one hand, then, I ask what particular forms of historical life could lead to the resounding 'Fuck life' of *Rockaby*, bearing in mind that the words are uttered by a particular character in a particular play, but that they also form part of a sustained and elaborated consistency, and are therefore more than just a 'point of view', and certainly more than an 'opinion'. On the other hand, I aim to write a minimalist biography that reduces what most people would think of as Beckett's life to a thin trickle between historical circumstance and art. This will not appeal to all tastes. But to those who wish to find out more, for example, about Beckett's relationships with Nancy Cunard or Alan Schneider, I thoroughly recommend Knowlson and Cronin. So, too, I shall seldom guess at Beckett's psychological states, other than as they are deducible from his writings. In intention, at least, like my minimalist approach, this constitutes a form of fidelity both to Beckett's own prioritization of his art, and to its methods.

At the same time, it by no means cuts the Gordian knot. The very agreement to write a biography, however far concerned to shrink the story itself and avoid any relapse into 'a wealth of filthy circumstance' (*TR*, p. 63), makes it impossible to quite disregard the man who lived. The question is rather how to establish a complex network of connections and disconnections between history, life and art. Some aspects of Beckett's life – his wanderings in Germany in 1936–7, for example, or in Vichy France in 1942 – seem to bring it close to the world of the works. Others seem to have little directly to do with it. Similarly, in certain respects, Beckett was and remained an example of the respectable Anglo-Irish and therefore in large part English middle-class virtues.

It is impossible to ignore this self-deprecating, reticent, disciplined, conscientious, diligent, implacably well-mannered, dauntingly forbearing person, not least because he appears in large measure to have been the origin of the myth of 'Saint Sam' amongst a generation of scholars who made his acquaintance. Since Steven Connor's ineffably bright and zestful deconstruction of the foundations of that myth, however, we have been less inclined to subscribe to it without *caveat*.[8] Much is sometimes made of Beckett the cricketer (the only Nobel Prize winner to have his name in Wisden). But gentleman Beckett was obsessed with his antithesis, the tramp. Look straight at the works themselves, and there is a great deal of material that – even insisting on the detachment of writer from narrator or character – simply does not square with the myth at all: the superciliousness and arrogance perceptible in the early writings, for example; the hysterical rage in the *Trilogy*; the extreme and sometimes murderous forms of violence from *Molloy* to *All That Fall* to *How It Is* and beyond.

Of course, to stress resistant features is not necessarily to discredit a hagiography. Quite the reverse: on the whole, they tend to make it more credible. Threats to saintliness raise the stakes. 'Oh it is not without scathe', says Moran, 'that one is gentle, courteous, reasonable, patient, day after day, year after year' (*TR*, p. 127). All the same, we are bound to wonder how far Beckett might have doggedly sustained a public persona quite distinct from the turbulent drives that were partly his inspiration, not least in order to protect their privacy. This is the implication of a quotation that he copied from Céline's *Mort à Crédit*, and that was clearly precious to him:

> L'essentiel c'est pas de savoir si on a tort ou raison, ça n'a vraiment pas d'importance . . . . Ce qu'il faut c'est décourager le monde qu'il s'occupe de vous . . . Le reste c'est du vice.[9]

In any case, as he himself says of the Dante he so revered, who wants to love Beckett? 'We want to READ' him (or see him performed, *DI*, p. 81).

That a writer with sensitivities as exquisite as Beckett's should have been cast into tumult is hardly surprising, given his historical experience. But here we encounter another problem. If Beckett seems to dissuade us from making smooth transitions back and forth between life and works, is the same not true, *a fortiori*, of transitions between works and historical contexts? Beckett asserted that a 'high, solitary art' was 'not to be clarified in any other light' than its own (*DI*, p. 145). He insisted on 'the acute and increasing anxiety' of *any* explicatory 'relation' (*DI*, p. 149). The artist who 'stakes his being', he wrote, 'is from nowhere, has no kith' (ibid.). This statement might seem to invalidate historical as much as biographical exegesis. Beckett was surely one of the great abstract modernists. To seek to bring his works back to historical fact is to tug in the opposite direction to his own. One might even argue that his direction is liberating, mine, imprisoning.

But freedom and constraint are not mutually exclusive. They define each other and are inseparable companions. Knowlson has exhaustively shown how many details from Beckett's life are present in his work. This does not comprehensively disprove Beckett's claim that life and art are distinct. But it hardly exactly bears it out, either. 'The danger is in the neatness of identifications', exact parallels: to affirm a precise correspondence between life and art may be a 'soothing' activity, 'like the contemplation of a carefully folded ham sandwich' (*DI*, p. 19). The correspondences are nonetheless not insignificant. What is true of the traces of biography in Beckett's art is also true of the traces of history. They neither allow us to establish a hard-and-fast relation between the works and historical circumstance nor absolutely deny the possibility of any such relation.

Indeed, in his writing about art, Beckett himself does not altogether eschew historical reflection. When, in his review of Albert

Feuillerat's book on Proust, he argues that Feuillerat seeks to restore to order the 'grave dissonances' and 'deplorable solutions of continuity' in Proust's great novel, he knows (and says) that these were the consequence of the First World War (*DI*, p. 63). Feuillerat's project is cosmetic, a scholarly endeavour to give a respectable appearance to a lacerated novel, to paint over historical scars. Or take a tiny poem:

Saint-Lô

vire will wind in other shadows
unborn through the bright ways tremble
and the old mind ghost-forsaken
sink into its havoc (*CP*, p. 32)

The theme appears to be spiritual chaos. But Saint-Lô is not just a place where personal disaster struck, like T. S. Eliot's Margate Sands ('On Margate Sands./ I can connect/ nothing with nothing').[10] Beckett's poem even functions as a critique of that kind of modernist indifference to the historical meaning of location. Saint-Lô is the capital of the *département* of La Manche in Normandy, and it was there that Beckett worked with the Irish Red Cross in 1945, the Vire being the river that runs through the city. In 1944, at the time of the Allied invasion of France, Saint-Lô had been a crucial objective in the breakout from the 'Normandy pocket' in which the attacking forces found themselves. Initially, they faced terrain that everywhere favoured the Germans. Past Saint-Lô, on the other hand, there would be much more freedom for manoeuvre. Hitler had therefore wanted the town stoutly defended. Allied progress was slow and bitter, and Saint-Lô suffered almost total devastation.[11] This was so much the case that some wished to leave the ruins intact, as historical testimony. Beckett's poem is partly about external 'havoc' (a word which originally referred to the battlefield).[12]

It even appears to respond to the debates about the future of Saint-Lô, turning, like the Vire, in a prophetic direction. At all events, 'Saint-Lô' presents the inner catastrophe as clearly determined by and inextricable from the outer one. It is about the relationship between the world of the mind and the historical world.

Few of Beckett's works, whether short or long, can be read in exactly this way. But, as we shall see, they are frequently marked in similar fashion by a biographically rooted historical consciousness, if often sporadically, fleetingly or here and there. It is such a historical consciousness on which this mini-biography will focus, rather than one that is the end-product of a more or less sophisticated, more or less novelistic psychologism (to which, we should add, Beckett himself was never remotely drawn).[13] At the same time, however, for all the ostensibly ahistorical character of much of Beckett's writing, it is above all *via* his works that the historical connection makes itself felt. To some people, this was always

'Total devastation': wartime damage to Saint-Lô, Normandy, August 1944.

obvious. Many of those alive when Beckett was writing, particularly after 1945, believed that he had an unusually profound grasp of the *zeitgeist*, and a power of conveying it unrivalled by any other contemporary artist. By now, however, it has become possible to give historical specificity and substance to that conviction; that is, we are by now far enough removed from the *zeitgeist* in question to get the measure of its historical closure. Indeed, like Yeats's, Joyce's and Woolf's before him, Beckett's death seemed both historical and logical, in that it was concurrent with the end of an era. If Beckett's works cannot simply be 'matched up' with historical contexts on the ham sandwich model, they are streaked by historical turmoils and the emotions provoked by them. Historical symptoms and effects weave their way across the rocky, unforgiving Beckettian surface like intermittent lodes of ore. Beckett's life took place in the small passageway between history and writing. I shall describe it accordingly.

That suggests that this short critical life will be somewhat patchy. It will indeed: here patchiness or intermittency becomes a method in itself. My book seeks to avoid resorting to global categories: the emphasis chiefly falls on discrete and discontinuous historical particulars. Beckett rejected the 'monde romancé that explains copious[ly] why e.g. Luther was inevitable without telling me anything about Luther, where he went next, what he lived on, what he died of, etc'.[14] I heed this rejection, even though I do not always conform exactly to its terms. Beckett wrote of the 'narrational trajectory' of Proust's *Recherche* that it was less like 'a respectable parabola' than 'the chart of an ague' (*DI*, p. 64). This life of Beckett aims to be such a chart. It therefore adduces history here and there, in fits and starts, as appearances and disappearances. It is a book of historical spasms, seizures, flushes and shivers, fevers and cold sweats. The Beckettian ague in large measure corresponded to the great *agon* of the world contemporary with it. But agues can be almost sprightly. They have their own intense, hectic vitality.

Patchiness will therefore be the rule. This is the case, not least in that this book simply leaves out many aspects of Beckett's life. Beckett distrusted all efforts to frame one sort of material with another quite distinct from it. They were threatened, he wrote, by 'the temptation to treat every concept "like a bass dropt neck fust in till a bung crate", and make a really tidy job of it' (*DI*, p. 19).[15] It is hard to avoid that trap. But I hope nonetheless to narrate Beckett's life, not as a *compte rendu* of pre-formed schemes, but as a *recherche*, a search, in all the complexity of 'its clues and blind alleys' (*DI*, p. 65).

Beckett's work involves such a search. More precisely, I take it to be an exploration of the possibilities of the 'event' from the vantage-point of the historical 'remainder'. I explained those two terms in my book *Beckett and Badiou*. That book might seem to point in a very different direction to this one. In fact, they are the same book. But *Beckett and Badiou* gives priority to the event, and is therefore necessarily abstract. This book is chiefly about the remainder, and is therefore an exercise in historical materialism. Together, however, they mimic the condition of our post-Derridean culture as trenchantly diagnosed by David Cunningham.[16] Under this condition, the historical world is hardly thinkable save on the basis of a transcendental principle which it has in fact determined from the start. We have no means of confronting, let alone proceeding on the basis of own acute and inescapable sense that we are everywhere and always historical beings. This paradox is decisive for the circle which the contemporary world seems condemned to tread. But what better to instruct us in the art of treading circles than the life and works of Samuel Beckett, after Dante and Joyce, perhaps the great master of the purgatorial form in art.

1

Arriving at an End: Ireland, 1906–28

Samuel Beckett was born in Foxrock, a select and eminently pros-
perous southern suburb of Dublin, in April 1906. He was of solidly
Protestant middle-class stock. His father, William, was quite probably
a descendant of Huguenot refugees fleeing religious persecution
in France in the late seventeenth century.[1] If so, however, the French
connection had long since ceased to count. William Beckett was
an affluent, successful building contractor. He became accustomed
to a certain milieu and style of life, climbing just about as high as
was possible for a scion of the Dublin Protestant bourgeoisie. The
Becketts' house, Cooldrinagh, was well-appointed, with quarters for
servants, a tennis court, lawns and a stable. William was a member
of the powerful, Protestant-dominated Freemasons and the exclusive Kildare Street Club, bastion of the Anglo-Irish and famous
for its aristocracy, claret and whist.

We should distinguish carefully between the Dublin Protestant
middle-classes and the landed Anglo-Irish.[2] But Beckett's mother,
May Roe, was of a family who had formerly been landowners.
Though the family had gone into decline, producing clergymen,
her father still held tenanted land. The class to which the Becketts
belonged identified with England, and tended to share the Anglo-
Irish gentry's conviction of their own superiority. They had little
or nothing to do with the Catholic majority, to whom their attitude
was condescending at best. Their unionism, 'their loyalty to the
Crown and the Union Jack' was 'automatic and unquestioning'.[3]

In his *German Diaries*, Beckett remembers a Union Jack handkerchief from his childhood (*GD*, 6.10.36). As we shall see, though loyalty was one of his more conspicuous traits, the Unionist adherence was not one that he was greatly concerned to sustain.

Unionist allegiances were not the only feature of his background which he was later to shrug off, or to which he was to prove indifferent. His parents themselves, however, certainly mattered to him. William seems to have loved his two sons, Frank, the elder, and Samuel, straightforwardly, and the feeling was straightforwardly reciprocated. May was religious, moody, turbulent, demanding. Samuel's relationship with her was complicated, and at times conflict-ridden, but there was obvious closeness in the torment, and she was to loom large in his psychic life for a very long time. When the poet John Montague asked him whether he had found much that was worthwhile on his journey through life, he singled out his mother and father, if in a characteristically sardonic tone, and in less than cheering terms. 'Precious little', he replied. 'And for bad measure, I watched both my parents die'.[4]

Beckett's educational career was not untypical of a product of his class. He went first to a genteel kindergarten near Cooldrinagh, where he mixed with children from very similar backgrounds to his own. Earlsfort House School, again in Foxrock, was equally respectable, but admitted Catholic children. However, his most significant early move was to Portora Royal School. Portora was in Enniskillen, in Northern Ireland. It was one of five Royal Schools. These had been founded in 1608, by Royal Charter, in the wake of the Tudor plantation of Ireland. James I's wish was that 'there shall be a free school at least in each county, appointed for the education of youth in learning and religion.'[5] In the event, five schools were established, providing an education to the sons of local merchants and farmers during the plantation of Ulster. They were sites for the production of a colonial class, enclaves of civilized value in the savage wilds. Portora eventually turned out large numbers of

'The Eton of Ireland': Portora Royal School, Enniskillen, Co. Fermanagh.

colonial administrators. Though diluted by the passage of time, the sense of purpose this involved still clung about the school that Beckett attended.

But Beckett began at Portora in 1920. Portora was sometimes known as 'the Eton of Ireland'. It had much of the ethos of an English public school. If the civilized virtue of the English presence in Ireland can ever be categorically distinguished from barbarism, 1920 was not a good year to try to do it. For Ireland was in the grip of the Anglo-Irish War. The New Year had begun with the recruitment of the Royal Irish Constabulary Reserve Force, otherwise known as the Black and Tans, followed (in July) by the 'Auxies', the Auxiliary Division of the RIC. Most of the recruits were British, many of them First World War army veterans. In Roy Foster's phrase, they behaved like 'independent mercenaries'.[6] Initially, at least, the Black and Tans were not subject to strict discipline, and avenged their losses by burning and sacking towns and villages and conducting arbitrary reprisals against the civilian population. The Auxies were if possible more brutal. Together with the Black and Tans, in December, they responded to an ambush by destroying Cork city centre. Thus ended a year that had also witnessed 'Bloody Sunday' (21 November), on which the Black and Tans had started firing into a football crowd. In Ulster itself and above all in Belfast, the year had also seen anti-Catholic pogroms.

Of course, the other side in the war also bore responsibility for its share of the general mayhem. But it did not preen itself on being one of the world's great civilizing powers. Nor did it come fully armed with institutions like Portora that boasted their commitment to 'honour, loyalty and integrity'.[7] Beckett had little respect for the kind of elite the school produced: when, for a very short spell in 1928, he taught at (the more recently founded, but similar) Campbell College, Belfast, he was critical of certain students. The then headmaster, William Duff Gibbon, MA, DSO, MC, suggested he remember that the boys at Campbell were 'the cream

Beckett in the Portora Royal School cricket team in 1923 (seated, at right).

of Ulster'. 'Yes, I know', retorted Beckett, 'rich and thick'.[8] His name does not appear in the old Campbellians' college history.

More importantly, like the writer who was to become his great mentor, Joyce, Beckett was painfully aware of the obscurity of any line supposedly demarcating civilization and barbarism, and wilfully blurred it in his work. The voice of the one insistently reverses into the voice of the other. Beckett's most illustrious predecessor at Portora was Oscar Wilde. However, he would not have found Wilde's name on the school honours board. It had been deleted after the scandal and trial of the 1890s. The school website still remarks on Wilde's infamy. The young Beckett was a fine sportsman, and seems to have accommodated himself quite smoothly to life at Portora. Yet his work amounts to a far more comprehensive assault on the spirit of Portora than Wilde's. Beckett's characters are remarkable for their lucid, disabused refusal to jack themselves up to flattering levels of self-deception. They owe some of their acrid tone and hilariously bleak clarity of vision to what Beckett saw around him in and after 1920, and the contradiction between Portora and its environment.

Portora had strong ties with Trinity College, Dublin. If Portora was a distinguished Anglo-Irish educational institution, TCD was the most eminent one. Founded in 1592 by Elizabeth I, it was the traditional university of the Protestant Ascendancy, Ireland's best (and for a long time its only) university institution. In principle at least, it had opened up to Catholics from 1794. But it did not feel open. The great Irish Catholic genius of his age, James Joyce, would not even have entered its superb library.[9] A gulf yawned between Trinity and the Catholic majority in Ireland, not least the Catholic intelligentsia, that was not merely religious, cultural and economic but also one of class. Some sense of what was at stake in this can be gleaned from J. P. Mahaffy's view of Joyce as 'a living argument in favour of my contention' that it was a mistake to establish a university 'for the aborigines of this island – for the corner boys that spit in the Liffey'.[10] In the early twentieth century, Mahaffy was one of the great Trinity luminaries, its Professor of Ancient History and, eventually, its Provost. He was a learned, gifted, eccentric and genuinely witty man. This did not save him from certain automatic responses, or the failures of intelligence they implied. Joyce and Beckett worked partly to destroy the assumptions underlying Mahaffy's 'contention', the one from without, the other from within.

Beckett attended TCD from 1923 to 1926. He went up to study for an Arts degree. Here he came under the influence of another imposing Trinity character, Thomas Rudmose-Brown, Professor of Romance Languages. In some ways, Rudmose-Brown rather resembled Mahaffy (though Mahaffy appears to have viewed him with some contempt). Rudmose-Brown was a snob who claimed a family coat of arms and royal descent, and vituperated against the consequences of Catholic majority rule. But he was also a wayward man, never really a member of the Trinity establishment. He was decisive for Beckett's development. Before Trinity, there was little or nothing in Beckett's Protestant background and education that might have nourished imagination or a speculative cast of mind. The claim that 'Rudmose-Brown made an intellectual out of a cricket-loving schoolboy' does not seem unduly extravagant.[11] The professor, whom Beckett referred to chiefly by his faintly Woosterish nickname of 'Ruddy', turned him in a vivifyingly un-Woosterish direction. For he particularly fostered Beckett's love not only of France, but of French intellect and French literature. In effect, he made it possible for Beckett to exchange one version of himself for another.

Rudmose-Brown, however, did not instil the will to change. This only gradually took hold of Beckett. But it had its roots in his social position in Ireland, and the historical circumstances that gave that position a very precise form at the time he was growing into adult-hood. The Anglo-Irish War came to an end with the signing of the

Anglo-Irish Treaty on 6 December 1922, and the birth of an independent Ireland. The trouble was that, for many, the new, independent Ireland was not independent enough. The Treaty granted Ireland only the freedom of a British dominion, gave Britain continuing rights in security and defence, and proposed a Boundary Commission that might pave the way to a permanent separation of Ulster from the Republic. The real sticking-point, however, was that the Treaty required an oath of allegiance to the British crown. This was too much for those who increasingly became known as the irreconcilables, notably Eamon de Valera. A split between 'Treatyites' and 'anti-Treatyites' was soon inevitable, and was followed by the Irish Civil War of 1922–3.

The Treatyites won. De Valera was arrested. William Cosgrave's government and party rapidly consolidated their power. Since the anti-Treatyites did not take up their seats in the Irish parliament, the government enjoyed considerable legislative authority. Of course, this tended to provoke resistance as much as quell it. There was an army mutiny, for example, in 1924. It was nonetheless clear that, whilst markedly reluctant to break with the political and administrative models of the old colonial master, the new government represented a triumph for the Catholic bourgeoisie and the patriots. It was also a triumph for the Roman Catholic church in Ireland. Whilst, as was traditional, the Church supported the government rather than those who dissented from it, for its part the State did not question the Church's authority in matters of health, education and sexual morality. Before long, the Irish government was passing singularly dismal laws on divorce, contraception and censorship. The Censorship of Films Act, with its restrictions on material 'unfit for general exhibition in public by reason of its being indecent, obscene or blasphemous', became law as early as 1923.[12] This was very much in line with the Church's proclamation that 'everything contrary to Christian purity and modesty' in modern cinema was alien to Catholic and Irish ideals,

'Contrary to Christian purity and modesty': an Irish demonstration in the 1920s.

as though the two were in principle one.[13] The same kind of thinking applied to literature, though Ireland did not get its Censorship of Publications Act until 1929.

In another of the greyly serendipitous moments with which Beckett's life seems punctuated, he returned from Northern Ireland in 1923, when it was about to become a haven of sorts for a residual, Protestant-dominated culture in Ireland, to the South, at a time when its Protestant culture was entering a final, twilit phase and the new Catholic culture was failing to offer any adequate replacement for it. Some Southern Protestants – W. B. Yeats, Andrew Jameson, Henry Guinness – were to play a very important part in the new Republic. But these were men of a very particular class or stamp and were already distinguished figures. In fact, Ireland had been leaking Protestants since before the First World War. The Anglo-Irish War and the Civil War only aggravated the trend. From the death of Parnell onwards, Protestant Ireland more or less consciously knew that it was playing an endgame, that the vector of history was no longer on its side. From 1923, it was clear that the power of Catholic nationalism, the Catholic bourgeoisie and the Catholic church was steadily growing and would continue to grow. The formation of the Irish Free State deprived the Beckett household of any politics 'except a silent and unexpressed loyalty to a regime which had vanished forever'. They therefore 'lived in a sort of political vacuum'.[14]

At the same time, however, in the period running from Beckett's birth in 1906 to his first major departure from Ireland in 1928, what Lionel Fleming called the question of 'identification' became crucial to the Anglo-Irish Protestant middle classes.[15] One of the recurrent themes of Dublin-suburban Protestant middle-class writings after 1922 – Fleming's *Head or Harp*, Terence de Vere White's *A Fretful Midge*, Patrick Campbell's *An Irishman's Diary*, Brian Inglis's *West Briton*, W. F. Casey's *The Suburban Groove*, Niall Rudd's *Pale Green, Light Orange*, Lennox Robinson's *The Big House* (a play) – is just how decisively the Anglo-Irish Houyhnhnms had separated themselves off from the Yahoos, how far they had asserted and confirmed their identity through militant segregation, or what Rudd calls 'an unstated system of "yes's" and "no's"'.[16] These people 'remained almost unaware of [the] other Ireland'.[17] Tramps often came to the Flemings' door, as they did to the Becketts', trying on old boots and trousers.[18] The door itself nonetheless marked a frontier between two worlds.

But the other Ireland 'was coming into its force'.[19] From 1922 onwards, the Protestant middle classes could hardly ignore this. They developed an increasingly uneasy if ambivalent sense of the need to make an effort, to bridge the gulf between the worlds. Undoubtedly, they frequently resented 'the State's effort to impose what to us was an alien culture'.[20] The young Beckett himself was occasionally capable of expressing this resentment. All the same, the distance that separated Anglo-Ireland from England was growing. By the late 1920s, Beckett's class might hate the new Irish national anthem, the Black and Tans, Gaelic sports, the Belfast bowler, de Valera and 'humbuggery' (the *vice anglais*) with equal vehemence.[21] As Robert ('Bertie') Smyllie, distinguished editor of the *Irish Times*, insisted, the Protestant middle class had to reach some kind of accommodation with the Free State.[22] Thus middle-class Protestants who remained in Ireland tended to experience a long, slow erosion of Anglo-Irish attitudes.

Beckett was to leave Ireland. This does not necessarily mean that his work is not partly an allegory of 'the process of [the] decay' of Anglo-Ireland,[23] or an allegory of Irish Protestant self-effacement and destitution after 1922. But the question of identification is most obviously crucial in his early collection of stories *More Pricks Than Kicks*. This is set in Dublin and focuses on Dublin milieux. It is concerned with the (intellectual, social and sexual) opportunities the city appears to offer (or fails to offer) to a clever young Protestant Irishman in a newly independent Ireland. The protagonist, Belacqua, is a Dublin, middle-class, Protestant intellectual. This places him in a profoundly equivocal position relative

Irish Protestant destitution: the ruins of a 'big house', 1923.

'La Mancha',
site of the 1926
'Malahide
murders'.

to Ireland in general and Dublin in particular. Heedlessly, with a quite conscious, deliberately cultivated indifference, the book freewheels among sometimes starkly contradictory positions.

Belacqua is deeply uncertain how far to shrug off the culture from which he stems. Take the first story in *More Pricks than Kicks*, 'Dante and the Lobster'. The figure of Henry McCabe, the so-called Malahide Murderer, is central to it. McCabe had worked as the gardener for a well-to-do family in Malahide, on the outskirts of Dublin, with two household staff. On 26 March 1926, he summoned the Civic Guard, telling them that the house was on fire. The Guard discovered the six bodies of the family and staff. The authorities deduced that the house had been set on fire intentionally, and the bodies showed traces of arsenic and violence.

McCabe was accused of the murders. His arrest, trial, and appeal caused a sensation in Ireland and received extensive press coverage. The evidence was at best inconclusive, and the prosecution's explanation of the accused's motives were ludicrously weak. Nonetheless, McCabe was sentenced to death. 'Dante and the Lobster' tells us that the sentence caused outrage, leading to a 'petition for mercy' which was 'signed by half the land' (*MPTK*, p. 17). This is doubtful. What is most important is that Beckett depicts the Ireland of 1926 as divided down the middle over a legal case involving capital punishment. For Irish republicans and nationalists were very much exercised by questions of the law in Ireland. Ireland had had an ancient legal system of its own, Brehon Law, which survived from the first English invasion in 1169 to the seventeenth century. From 1169 onwards, however, it was increasingly replaced by the colonizer's law, Crown Law, and the British system of judicial procedures, procedures for the establishment of guilt and innocence and for punishment, including capital punishment.

In dissident and nationalist Ireland, however, there persisted a conviction of the foreignness of British law, the fact that it had been imposed on an unwilling people. This conviction was much enhanced by nineteenth-century historians, antiquarians and scholars, who rediscovered Brehon Law. This led to the creation of a Brehon Law Commission which produced *Ancient Laws of Ireland*, a six-volume set which made it possible to understand what Irish legal tradition had been before colonization, and therefore to imagine what it might have been without the colonial presence. In particular, as opposed to Crown Law, Brehon Law had had no state-sponsored system of enforcement. The issue over which Ireland was most divided in the 1920s was how far it ought to throw over, to finish with the presence of English traditions, and allegiance to the British Crown. The question of continuing with a state-administered death penalty was a question of adherence to Crown Law. Broadly speaking, to call British legal tradition into question was nationalist, to defend it a position identifiable with the English in Ireland, including Beckett and Belacqua's class.

It is thus no accident that *More Pricks Than Kicks* begins with a question involving Crown Law. Henry McCabe died on Thursday, 9 December 1926. 'Dante and the Lobster' is set on 8 December. The story traces Belacqua's conversion to a position on the death penalty that is strictly more of a nationalist than an Anglo-Irish one. At the beginning of the story, Belacqua is sufficiently indifferent to MacCabe to cut into a loaf of bread on his picture in the newspaper. By the end of the story, by contrast, he has grown more rueful:

> And poor McCabe, he would get it in the neck at dawn. What was he doing now, how was he feeling? He would relish one more meal, one more night. (*MPTK*, p. 20)

'Mercy in the stress of sacrifice, a little mercy to rejoice against judgment' (ibid.): this is the emphasis on which the story ends. In ending it thus, however discreetly, Beckett calls into question a philosophy of law bequeathed to a newly independent Ireland by its colonizer.

But if, at the end of the story, we see a Belacqua shrugging off one of the habits of thought more or less automatic in his class, elsewhere, we see him abundantly continuing in those habits. Furthermore, his sympathy for McCabe is itself finally ambivalent. He can properly feel for a creature abruptly thrust into sudden death only in the instance of a living lobster about to be boiled, on to which he displaces any nascent emotions he may feel on McCabe's behalf. Indeed, in the very last line, Beckett himself even has to correct Belacqua's responses. Belacqua shrugs off the impulse to care: 'Well . . . it's a quick death, God help us all'. To which his author retorts, smartly, 'It is not' (*MPTK*, p. 21). Belacqua is finally non-committal, lukewarm, and therefore mired in unimportance.

In the late 1920s, Belacqua is placed in a profoundly equivocal position relative to Ireland by virtue of being a middle-class Protestant intellectual. There is a good deal of fun, in *More Pricks Than Kicks*, at the expense of the Anglo-Irish Revival's literary stock-in-trade. But if Belacqua treats various features of Anglo-Irish revivalist culture with scorn, he is equally dismissive of the new national culture. The name of Patrick Pearse half puts him off the 'most pleasant street' that bears it (*MPTK*, p. 43). Law and order

are maintained by brutish Civic Guards. One of the dominant
features of newly independent Dublin is its 'Star of Bethlehem',
advertising that notable British export, Bovril (*MPTK*, p. 53). The
narrator adds that philistines have clamped a 'glittering vitrine'
over the Perugino Pietà in the National Gallery (*MPTK*, p. 93). Faced
with a historical fiasco, it is not surprising to find Belacqua hoping
that Trinity College will endure in perpetuity. In the nooks and
crannies of *More Pricks Than Kicks*, there lurks a sense of a catastrophic history that will equally haunt Beckett's later work. Here,
however, the catastrophe is chiefly indicated in the catastrophic
inability of the present to come to any kind of significant terms
with historical catastrophe. Thus Dublin is 'the home of tragedy
restored and enlarged' (ibid.).

Belacqua is both inclined and disinclined to shrug off the culture from which he stems. This ambivalence is endemic to the book.
More than anything else, Belacqua is unserious. For he inhabits a
cultural no man's land. Belacqua's women, his marriages and affairs
have the same quality of indeterminacy (or lack of determination)
about them. This sexual Laodiceanism is not only a principal theme
in the long unpublished predecessor to *More Pricks Than Kicks*,
but is also precisely conveyed in (if hardly mitigated by) the arch-
ness of its title, *Dream of Fair to Middling Women*. In the later text,
however, Belacqua's relationships exemplify a range of choices that
are sexual and cultural together: Winnie the good young Protestant
bourgeoise, Lucy the Ascendancy horsewoman, Thelma one of
the rising class of the Dublin petit bourgeoisie, Ruby the Irishtown
working-class girl, the Smeraldina the exotic foreigner. This is
partly a reflection of Beckett's own situation during the twenties and
early thirties. He fell amateurishly in love with Ethna MacCarthy,
a magnetically attractive fellow student at Trinity College (later to
marry his good friend Con Leventhal). He fell romantically in love
with his half-Jewish cousin Peggy Sinclair, whose family had moved to
Germany. Later, in Paris, he had a somewhat ambivalent if clearly not

sexual relationship with Joyce's daughter Lucia. Other women featured more or less significantly within the Beckettian psychodrama.

Beckett extracts certain features of his own early experience with women and injects them into *More Pricks Than Kicks*. But he also makes them Irish-focussed. He works on a principle that will repeatedly be evident in his later work: he organizes the indeterminacy of his own experience, but as indeterminacy. He abstracts Belacqua's inchoate emotional life, but as drift. He produces a version of the long-established Irish tradition of allegorizing women. But he also treats this predominantly nationalist tradition ironically, making it serve purposes for which it was never intended, whilst expanding it, too. He makes it express, not the aspirations of what were by now the victorious classes in Ireland, but the desperations of a historically defeated and obsolescent class. The full range of the choices finally available to Belacqua matters little. The point

'These old crones, Ireland is full of them'.

is that 'the forces' in Belacqua's mind will 'not resolve' (*MPTK*, p. 136). He makes no decisive choice. He has been deprived of any cultural foundation that might make such an act of self-definition possible. All his women are in some sense equivalent, because nothing of itself defines Belacqua in relation to them. Choice itself implodes, and Belacqua's death arrives inconsequentially, at the random end of what is, in principle, an indefinitely extendable series.

In the long run, Beckett's work was to take a quite different direction to *More Pricks than Kicks*. It would bear a different kind of witness to the readjustment that, from 1922 onwards, the Dublin Protestant middle classes increasingly found themselves constrained to make.[24] But this is a drably clinical way of evoking a magisterially traumatized and impotent art. By and large, Beckett's class had either exploited, patronized or ignored those subjected to a condition of ancient dispossession and deprivation. After *More Pricks than Kicks*, however, Beckett himself is more and more powerfully drawn towards identifying with the historical lament of the 'other Ireland'. His childhood world was crammed with insubstantial presences, in the sense that it was full of people who didn't count, who were not supposed to matter: the itinerant beggars, the tinkers in the back roads of Foxrock, the slummy stonecutters of nearby Glencullen. He declared of the maddened woman in his play *Not I* that 'there were so many of these old crones, stumbling down the lanes, in the ditches, beside the hedgerows. Ireland is full of them'.[25] His childhood had left him 'aware of the unhappiness' of others around him.[26] He saturated his work in this unhappiness.

The Protestant middle classes had refused to assume any historical responsibility for the other Ireland. Beckett can hardly be said to assume it, either. But it nags away insidiously within his characters' monologues and speeches. He was far too scrupulous and too subtle to imagine that any true 'identification' with the other Ireland was finally possible. There was therefore 'nothing to be done' (*CDW*, p. 11); nothing, that is, save accept a certain 'obligation to express' (*DI*, p. 139). True, in Beckett, expression breeds suppression. Lucky's majestically nonsensical monologue in *Waiting for Godot* is so compulsive that, in the end, the other characters have violently to floor him. But the obligation to express implacably reasserts its hold. The claim of the other voice can never be stilled, because its historical condition leaves it beyond all possibility of being appropriated. It is, par excellence, 'Not I'.

'When it's over, ma'am', said the maid to de Vere White's mother of the upheavals in Ireland in the twenties, 'yous will be us and us will be yous'.[27] As history repeatedly showed and Beckett was acutely aware, this was not to be. It is Kate's vain hope in *The Big House*. She learns that 'the gulf remain[s]' and is absolutely unbridgeable.[28] If she is to stay and commit herself to Ireland, she must do so in that knowledge. If she finds any new identity for herself, it will be partial and incomplete. Beckett's interests are very different to Kate's.[29] But he expresses the same point as she does, perhaps above all, in Hamm's impatient repudiations of others' suffering in *Endgame*. In so far as *Endgame* can be thought of as alluding to Ireland – we will encounter a different way of reading it later – Hamm's mixture of misery and callousness is a double irony directed at the hypocrisy of a class for whom, in Inglis's phrase, the 'other Irish' were 'a people to extol in conversation around a tea table, but still savages'.[30] Hamm has no truck with the trivial, self-cleansing fantasy that one might atone for historical suffering by proclaiming one's solidarity with the oppressed. For Beckett, any concept of finding a new identity for himself within Irish culture was bound to be acutely problematic. Not surprisingly, he looked elsewhere.

2

Not Worth Tuppence: Paris and the École Normale Supérieure, 1928–30

Beckett performed extremely well in Trinity College's School of Modern Languages. He became Rudmose-Brown's favourite student. Early in 1927, Rudmose-Brown suggested that he allow his name to be put forward as Trinity College's exchange lecturer in English for the coming year at the École Normale Supérieure in Paris. In the event, the man he was supposed to replace, Thomas MacGreevy, clung on for another year, and Beckett was not in the post until November 1928. He arrived to find MacGreevy still occupying his room.

MacGreevy even contrived to stay at the École Normale for another couple of years, during which he and Beckett embarked on what would turn out to be a lifelong friendship. MacGreevy's reluctance to be squeezed out is understandable enough. He was a poet with serious intellectual appetites and a love of modern art. In 1928 there was nowhere better to be than the *rive gauche*. Beckett himself quickly saw what it might offer. In Paris in *Dream of Fair to Middling Women*, Belacqua spends his money on 'concerts, cinemas, cocktails, theatres, apéritifs' (notably 'the potent unpleasant Mandarin-Curaçao' and 'the ubiqitous Fernet-Branca . . . like a short story by Mauriac to look at', *DFMW*, p. 37). Beckett behaved in a similar fashion. He also began an enduring habit of visiting art galleries. It was to his first years in Paris that he owed his growing interest in the avant-garde and his involvement in avant-garde circles. In the Paris of the late 1920s, the Surrealists were in full cry. The little magazines were going from strength to strength.

These included Eugene Jolas's *transition*, which was publishing Joyce's *Work in Progress*. It would eventually serve as Beckett's first publisher, notably in the case of his short story, 'Assumption'.

That Beckett met Joyce had nothing to do with any arcane law of irresistible forces impelling two pioneering modernists towards one another. It was more a question of Irish connections. Beckett admired Joyce and his work before he got to Paris. He arrived with a letter of introduction from his uncle Harry Sinclair, who had known Joyce in Dublin. But the instrumental figure was MacGreevy. By the late 1920s, Joyce had surrounded himself with an established group of friends, amongst whom the Irish held a special place. The friends were also a support team: they put themselves at his disposal, kept him company on his outings, went on errands and performed little tasks for him. At his behest, they even looked after other friends. Above all, they worked as amanuenses and researchers for 'Work in Progress', reading books for Joyce and reporting back to him. With Brian Coffey and Arthur Power, MacGreevy was one of a small group of younger Irish writers and poets who were now congregating around the great man, and sometimes contributing to his project.

MacGreevy brought Beckett into Joyce's orbit. Before very long, Beckett, too, was functioning as a kind of research assistant on the project that would eventually be known as *Finnegans Wake*. Indeed, Joyce obviously spotted part at least of the young man's potential distinction, for he quickly invited him to write an essay for the volume *Our Exagmination round his Factification for Incamination of Work in Progress*. It turned out to be the most illuminating and arrestingly written of the twelve contributions, though it sheds light quite as much on what were to become Beckettian preoccupations as it does on Joyce's.

Whether or not a mutual recognition of spiritual kinship was at stake, then, the relationship began very promisingly. It did not continue in the same vein. In 1928–30, Joyce's daughter Lucia had yet to descend into the mental and psychological disarray that would so harrow her (and her family) in the 1930s. Since Beckett had become a family friend, it was logical that the two of them should be rather thrown together. Apart from meeting him in the Joyces' apartment, she would call on him in the École Normale, and they would go out together. Since they sometimes appeared as a couple, that was what others took them for. Lucia was inclined to take them for one, too; at the very least, she clearly imagined that coupledom might be just around the corner. But Lucia was already showing signs of volatility, and Beckett's devotion was to Joyce himself. Haplessly, clumsily, with more than a touch of what, shortly afterwards, he would call 'the loutishness of learning' (*CP*, p. 7), the young man disabused the daughter. The pain Lucia suffered was extreme. In a fury, Joyce barred Beckett from any further contact with himself and his family. As he discovered the full extent of Lucia's predicament, he would gradually relent. For the moment, however, Beckett was left with the dismaying conviction that he had betrayed the trust, not just of a great modern writer, but a man he thought of as a 'heroic being' and fit object of reverence.[1]

To focus on this 'Left Bank Beckett', however, is to narrate the beginnings of his French career from a familiar perspective whose very currency gives one reason to doubt it: the great modernist-to-be swiftly establishes himself within an international, cosmopolitan, avant-gardist crowd which is where, of course, he naturally belonged.[2] Joyce, above all, is his passport both to international modernism and a world where, in Robert McAlmon's phrase, everyone was busy 'being geniuses together'.[3] The piece may fit into the picture rather awkwardly: Beckett is nothing if not a melancholic modernist, and therefore something of a fringe figure, ill at ease. He haunts the milieu, rather than being at its centre. All the same, it is where he belongs. But his dislike for quite a lot of expatriate modernists, from Hemingway (as a man) to Wyndham Lewis (as a writer), is merely one of a number of aspects of Beckett that do not quite square with this conception of him. In any case, there was more than one culture on the Left Bank.

Unlike other expatriates, Beckett was to settle in Paris for good. He also immersed himself in both the language and the culture. At length, he became as much French as he was Irish. His partner and many of his closest friends were French. Beckett was not a deracinated figure in the sense that, say, Pound was, and did not lead a deracinated life in the sense that Pound did. He was a man of strong loyalties, who put down roots, if rather eccentrically. He rooted himself in Paris as other expatriates did not. In particular, at a time when he still saw himself as a university man rather than a writer, he spent two years living and working in the École Normale Supérieure.

The École Normale is quite distinct from the other great university institutions in Paris. It was born of the Revolution, on the ninth Brumaire, Year III (30 October 1794). Joseph Lakanal, one of its co-founders, announced that it was to be a source of pure and abundant light. Dominique Joseph Garat, disciple of Condorcet and its second co-founder, declared that it embodied an educational project possible 'for the first time on earth', to wit, 'the regeneration of human understanding' in a society of equals.[4] According to baron and statesman Prosper de Barante, its goal was the transformation of 'the laws of reason and intelligence' themselves.[5] In more practical terms, Garat and Lakanal also wanted it to create not only an Enlightenment-oriented intelligentsia, but a national elite and a cadre of teachers for the new republic. Heady, adventurous, chaotic, it was quickly suppressed, but Napoleon revived it. The intake of the new institution, however, was small, marked out by merit and subject to quasi-military discipline.

The ensuing history of the institution exactly captures its spirit. Its fortunes depended on political regimes. After the Restoration in 1814, it soon became suspect again, as a 'nest of liberalism' fomenting 'a spirit of insubordination',[6] and was suppressed once more. With the July Revolution in 1830, it made a swift comeback, but the Second Empire distrusted it. Minister of Education Hippolyte

Fortoul aimed 'to lower [its] level of intellectual sophistication'.[7] He duly presided over the collapse of philosophy into logic, the disappearance of history teaching, a reduction of library hours and the introduction of government spies in classrooms. Not surprisingly, the École Normale once more declined into relative obscurity.

By no means necessarily given to revolutionary politics – in 1848, most of them enlisted in the Garde Nationale, and opposed the revolutionary cause – the *normaliens* nonetheless repeatedly proved their republican credentials by turning orthodoxies on their heads and defying institutional constraints and repressive measures. Above all, they asserted the principle of intellectual independence, of what

Normaliens taking to the roofs of the École Normale Supérieure, as was traditional.

normalien Jean Giraudoux was to call 'the particularly and passion-
ately individual life'.[8] The École Normale developed an implicit
code of moral judgement which indeed sought to function as
though it were in existence 'for the first time on earth'. It was
'normal' proleptically, in hope. Thus, whilst not always or even
frequently of the Left, *normaliens* were almost invariably hated
by the official right. They also responded splendidly to the great
French moral crises of the nineteenth century, notably in the case
of Dreyfus in the 1890s.

The École Normale produced a series of eminent figures, from
Michelet and Cousin in the 1830s to Pasteur, to Bergson and Jaurès
in the 1870s, Durkheim in the 1880s and Blum and Péguy in the
1890s. The figure, however, who perhaps loomed largest at the
modern École Normale was Lucien Herr, polyglot, polymath,
socialist, man of deep principle and librarian *extraordinaire*. It
was Herr who, on Dreyfus's behalf, leapt on his bicycle to awaken
the conscience of *normaliens*. Herr was a profound influence on
the École Normale that Beckett knew, dying just two years before
Beckett arrived. Another was Ernest Lavisse. Under the direction
of Lavisse (1904–19), the ethos of the École Normale became one
of anarchic freedom, with virtually no discipline. *Normaliens* of
the 1920s would walk on the rooftops long into the night, go out
for drinks in their pyjamas, dangle their feet in the goldfish pond
and squat in three-franc cinemas on the Avenue des Gobelins
watching Buster Keaton and Harold Lloyd.[9] Beckett captures
something of the tone in the Parisian passages in *Dream of Fair
to Middling Women*, when the Wagnerite Liebert wears plus fours
to a performance of *Die Walküre* (only to be refused entry: '"Go
home" they said gently, "and get out of your cyclist's breeches"',
DFMW, p. 37). So, too, the École Normale was a magnet for idiosyncratic talent. André Maurois, René Clair and Tristan Tzara all
paid visits. The emphasis, above all, was on unfettered intellectual
development in its own lights and for its own sake.

Indeed, in the 1920s, the École was a 'brilliant and animated' if increasingly dilapidated institution.[10] Aron, Nizan, Sartre, Merleau-Ponty, Simone Weil, Lautman, Canguilhem and Cavaillès all attended during this decade. Add the names of later luminaries, and the roll-call of intellectual honour is staggering: Césaire, Lévy-Bruhl, Althusser, Foucault, Derrida, Badiou, Rancière . . . The list is by no means exhaustive, and dwarfs other, comparable lists. Anglophone Beckett scholars sometimes play down the importance of the École Normale in his life. The same cannot be said of *normaliens*, who regularly claim him as one of their own. That fact should not be slighted. Since both Francophone and Anglophone sides have their own kind of authority, the contradiction in itself tells us something very important about Beckett and his *œuvre*.

The products of the École Normale made much of the famous *esprit normalien*. They were especially proud of their humorous

The 'celebrated generation of 1924' at the École Normale Supérieure included Nizan, Péron and Sartre.

view of life. *Normaliens* positively sought out antitheses. They made a virtue of chronic (and comic) inconsistency. Before he joined the Party in 1926, for example, Paul Nizan contrived to be an arch-conservative defender of the Church, committed Communist, dandy and avant-gardist, all at the same time.[11] The *esprit normalien* particularly manifested itself in the *canular*, an often extremely elaborate form of witty, ironical, practical joke. According to Alain Peyrefitte, it was 'the very symbol' of the place itself.[12] *Canulars* could be Pantagruelian or Ubuesque. They revelled in paradox and outrageous contradiction, wresting sense from nonsense, luxury from decrepitude, intellectual wealth from poverty and filth.[13] They deceived by intention. Some of the most successful ones were virtually indistinguishable from serious intellectual endeavours. Alternatively, serious concerns shaded into *canulars.* Bourbaki eventually became the collective signifier of a major group of mathematicians. But it was originally the name of a mysterious bearded figure who appeared in a lecture-room one day and bewildered a group of hapless first-years with an entirely spurious disquisition. At moments like this, the École Normale of the twenties seemed to be a Carrollian world where learning was scarcely separable from its naughty double, and parodic forms of intellectual discourse might actually anticipate their more serious versions.

But there was also an extremely serious side to the *normaliens*' self-image that was almost the reverse of *canular* humour, an ethical limit at which flinty inflexibility abruptly became imperative. Françoise Proust calls this the 'granite point'.[14] The 'granite point' was the point at which one stuck and absolutely refused to budge. It involved intellectual principle, and required demanding and even extreme forms of consistency. Herr and the Dreyfusards provided an inspiring example of this. The *normaliens*' 'brilliant record in the Resistance' offers a later one.[15] True, *normaliens* collaborated, too; the École Normale always had its right.[16] Nonetheless, it was left and liberal *normaliens* who were chiefly responsible for its reputation.

Their implacable pursuit of their causes, often to the disgrace of a more official culture, lent them enormous prestige. The Sartrian concept of *engagement* self-evidently belongs within this tradition.

The traditions of the *canular* and the 'granite point' had one feature in common: both were affirmations of the power and autonomy of the intellect, triumphs of the mind over ordinary circumstance. Robert Brasillach described the École Normale as an astonishing haven 'of poetic anarchy . . . a fragile masterpiece of freedom'.[17] When Beckett's Murphy asserts that a factual resolution to a problem may resolve it, but 'only in fact' (*MU*, p. 101), he sounds close to the culture from which Cavaillès learnt the importance of not accepting facts, 'for, after all, they are only facts'.[18] Georges Pompidou (of all people) thought of the École Normale as offering a kingdom not of the world but of the spirit.[19] In effect, the Idea came first. This would also be the case with Beckett; and if it was so in a weirdly distinctive way, then that was *normalien* too.

It is extremely unlikely that Beckett spent any time at the École Normale discussing phenomenology with Merleau-Ponty (though Husserl lectured in Paris in 1929).[20] Nor did he engage in earnest conversations with Sartre, of a kind in which a prescient eavesdropper might have detected the first small seeds of existentialism. They would have been more likely to talk about Synge and James Stephens, whom Sartre was enthusiastically reading at the time.[21] But whilst certainly rather detached, Beckett was not a solitary figure on the edge of the institution. He had two particular friends there, Georges Pelorson and Jean Beaufret, neither of whom were marginal figures, both of whom belonged to particular circles of *normaliens* and appear routinely in others' memoirs. Beckett continued to see Pelorson after his time at the École. Since 1926, he had also been friends with Alfred Péron, a *normalien* whom he had first met at Trinity in 1926, and who first introduced him to various aspects of *normalien* culture. Péron had been a friend (since school) of Nizan and Sartre, who had an affair with his cousin. He was later to take on an austere and finally a sombre significance in Beckett's life.

Beckett's interest in continental philosophy began at the École, which is where he became a serious reader of it.[22] In the Parisian section of *Dream of Fair to Middling Women*, Lucien quotes one of the *normaliens'* classic points of philosophical reference, Leibniz's account of the infinitesimal structure of matter.[23] Material traces of *normalien* culture also flicker here and there in Beckett's work. Lucky's extravagantly absurd monologue in *Waiting for Godot* may owe a debt to *canulars*: figures with ropes around their necks certainly recurred in them. If 'pseudo-couples' throng Beckett's works, they were also around in the École Normale. Sartre and Nizan, for example, were so close as to be popularly known as Nitre and Sarzan. *Normaliens* also had a special argot, and Beckett, with his gargantuan appetite for language, was no doubt aware of it. The French word 'pot', for example, the English form of which so exercises Beckett's Watt, had so many different meanings at the École as to leave *normaliens* themselves scratching their heads. The word 'clou', on which the name of one of the two principal characters in *Endgame* is often thought to be a pun, was a key term in *normalien* slang. A *normalien* was a *cloutier*, meaning he wasn't worth tuppence ('il ne vaut pas un clou').[24] *Normaliens* had a particular taste for self-deprecation: this, again, was an affair of intellectual honour. The young Beckett was both temperamentally and culturally disposed to self-effacement. This disposition would later produce a writing remarkable for its extraordinarily subtle dismantlings of the ego. It was doubtless reinforced by the École.

But above all, the spirit of the *canular*, its irreducible, wry irony, its reverse injection of wild inventiveness, was clearly important for Beckett. Few features of his literary, philosophical and cultural experience seem closer to his intricately, bizarrely, endemically ironical cast of mind than the *canular*. Early in 1931, after returning from Paris, as part of the annual presentation of the Modern Languages

Society at Trinity, in what was obviously a fit of nostalgia for the *esprit normalien*, he and Pelorson staged *Le Kid*, a one-act burlesque of Corneille's *Le Cid*. *Le Kid* was 'an intellectual "canular"'.[25] *Normalien* playfulness, however, did not go down well everywhere in Trinity. Rudmose-Brown, in particular, was hugely infuriated.

Just a couple of months before this, Beckett had also given a paper on 'Le Concentrisme' to the Modern Languages Society that Ruby Cohn describes as recognizably 'a *canular normalien*' (*DI*, p. 10). To start with, it appears to be a casual skit on modern movements and the manifestos promoting them. It delights in surrealist extravagance and inconsequence, and pours out a stream of more or less mystifying definitions. Thus where Stendhal classically defined the novel as a mirror carried down a highway, Beckett's Jean du Chas declares that '*concentrism is a prism on a staircase*' (*DI*, p. 41). There are hints of Poundian tirade in the paper, laced with the appropriate obscurities and a dash of Eliot: 'Under the crapulous aegis of a Cornelian valet the last trace of Dantesque rage is transformed into the spittle of a fatigued Jesuit. . . . Montaigne bears the name of Baedeker, and God wears a red waistcoat' (*DI*, p. 39). The paper dismisses a vast expanse of cultural history, particularly the nineteenth century, with a negligent grandeur that also calls certain modernist self-promotions in mind.

However, the paper doesn't really focus on Concentrism. Firstly, it is more concerned with what one might putatively call the Life and Thought of Jean du Chas and their eccentricities. Secondly, its baroque and elaborate form is not that of a manifesto. The main document appears to be composed by a third party who is addressed, in a prefatory letter, by a second party whom du Chas accosted in a bar in Marseilles, and to whom he finally left his papers. It is not clear that the addressee of the letter and the third party are in fact one person. With some justification, Cohn sees 'Le Concentrisme' as mocking 'pedantry' or learning (*DI*, p. 10), 'the reduction of [du Chas's] substance to university hiccups [*hoquets universitaires*]' (*DI*, p. 41). But here again there are problems: the form of the piece is not that of a mock-learned essay but a biographical sketch. The presentation of the piece is not scholarly, and nor is its learning. It is, again, more Poundian than that: rich, individual, diverse, unpedantic but untidy. So, too, the presentation of the materials is modernistic: 'Le Concentrisme' provides us with an elegantly tiered narration, a structure of boxes within boxes with complicating points of indeterminacy, like Gide's *Les Faux-Monnayeurs*. Gide is a repeated point of reference, and du Chas keeps a Gide-like journal.

There are even difficulties with thinking of 'Le Concentrisme' as a *canular*: quintessentially, the *canular* was a hoax. It hoodwinked people. Beckett does not appear to have seriously intended a deceit, and no-one at the Modern Languages Society was taken in.[26] But a strain of the *canular* runs deep in the paper. Firstly, a multiplication of forms of irony was typical of the more sophisticated *canulars*; so, too, in 'Le Concentrisme', the irony turns both outward and inward. Like *canulars*, the piece delights in contradicting itself. The Gide to whom it might seem to pay substantial homage is casually dismissed in the middle of it. Similarly, its offhand non-sequiturs overflow any satirical purpose, expressing a pervasive indifference to logical criteria, if not despairing of them. The result is a minor instance of a form of irony that has haunted European tradition at least since Erasmus, an irony without foundations, spinning on itself like a whirligig in a void. *Canular* irony was like this. However much Beckett inherited from a vertiginously ironic tradition in Anglo-Irish literature supremely exemplified in Swift and Sterne, he also owed a debt to the *normaliens*.

There is a third example of the influence of the *canular* on Beckett: not long before 'Le Concentrisme', in June 1930, he composed a work that the paper seems quite often to echo, the poem 'Whoroscope'. He wrote it for a competition sponsored by two figures prominent in the Parisian avant-garde, McAlmon and Nancy Cunard, and the poem effectively connected the two Left Bank cultures with which he was familiar. In effect, Beckett exploited what the École Normale was able to give him for avant-garde purposes. At first sight, 'Whoroscope' looks like a patently modernist piece of work. Its sports a set of endnotes, for example, purporting to explain some of its more obscure allusions, which obviously calls T. S. Eliot's 'The Waste Land' to mind. Indeed, the poem itself is rather like a collection of notes, consisting largely of scraps from source-texts, if in radically attenuated form. Here Beckett's working method appears to resemble Joyce's, or Pound's in the *Cantos*.

But this is to fit the poem into a ready-made frame. 'Whoroscope' won the competition. If it met with success outside the École Normale, however, the poem was very much composed within it. Matthew Feldman has recently shown that Beckett's drew on source-texts that were either in the École Normale library, or that he borrowed from Beaufret.[27] Furthermore, the subject of the poem is the life of Descartes. In other words, it addresses a philosopher of towering importance within École Normale culture. Of course, the significance of Descartes in the École Normale during the 1920s is hardly a simple matter. In the late nineteenth and early twentieth century Gabriel Monod, Joseph Bédier and Gustave Lanson had achieved 'official recognition' for various aspects of the Cartesian tradition within the École,[28] and this persisted into the 1920s. The young Sartre, for example, was an enthusiastic Cartesian.[29] At the same time, however, those who espoused Cartesian tradition repeatedly collided with defenders of Pascalian sensibility and promoters of Bergsonian anti-rationalism. Nonetheless, according to Robert Smith, a Cartesian insistence on 'the priority and independence of the mind remained the central strand' of the École Normale's tradition 'throughout the Third Republic'.[30] This was the case, not least, because of the work of Léon Brunschvicg, who was using Cartesianism as the foundation for a new idealism, particularly in the 1920s. Yet *normaliens* also treated Descartes with their customary irreverence. In *Dream of Fair to Middling Women*, Lucien tells stories 'about the grouch of Descartes against Galileo' that are 'mostly of his own invention' (*DFMW*, p. 47). Singing *chansons* with lyrics by Descartes was a favourite pastime. In other words, Descartes was by no means exempt from the spirit of the *canular*.

Feldman has superbly demolished a tradition in Beckett studies which discovered a protracted engagement with Cartesian thought in his work. He demonstrates convincingly that Beckett's knowledge of Descartes was 'cursory' and that he 'generally sought out synoptic secondary sources'.[31] 'Whoroscope' is the one Beckett text 'indisputably created with Cartesian sources to hand'.[32] In other words, Beckett's treatment of Descartes in the poem is precisely historical. Firstly, with 'Le Concentrisme', it belongs to a period when he is meditating ironically on the form of the short life (which incidentally makes both of interest to anyone trying to write one). Secondly, it positions itself in relation to a highly contested and in large part contemporary terrain.

For if Beckett's poem draws heavily on his sources for its detail, it also radically departs from their larger theses regarding the meaning of Cartesianism. J. P. Mahaffy, no less, had written a book on Descartes, and Beckett seems to have discovered it in the École Normale library (if he did not know about it already). Whilst Mahaffy could hardly turn Descartes into a Protestant, he nonetheless placed him in the vanguard of a modernity that he also associated with Protestantism. By contrast, Adrien Baillet's classic *La vie de Monsieur Des-Cartes* (1691) – much scorned by Mahaffy, but still cited today, by Rancière among others[33] – presented Descartes as a good, faithful, practising Catholic. Furthermore, if Beckett read Volume 12 of Descartes's *Œuvres complètes*, Charles Adam's biography, which Lawrence Harvey took to be important for 'Whoroscope',[34] he would have encountered a Descartes much more central to and in tune with the École Normale (and which he would have therefore been much more likely to encounter anyway): an Enlightenment man, revolutionary philosopher of progress and founder of modern science.

Beckett's Descartes is none of these figures. On the surface of things, his irreverence towards the Mass might make him seem closest to Mahaffy's version. But Descartes' most beautiful lines in a notably un-beautiful poem actually evoke Dante's God. The biggest influence on Beckett's life of Descartes is none of his sources, but Stephen Dedalus's life of Shakespeare in *Ulysses* (which it echoes). Beckett sharply demystifies Descartes, as Stephen does Shakespeare. His positions often seem wilfully heterodox, like Stephen's. Where the standard account makes of Descartes a man, above all, of 'powerfully linked ideas',[35] Beckett's 'biography' of him is diffuse and marked by inconsequence. The poem is itself strikingly un-Cartesian, above all, in its inconsistencies. Certainly, as a recklessly un-Cartesian life of Descartes, it looks very like a *canular*.

However, there are further levels of irony in 'Whoroscope'. If Baillet, Mahaffy and Adam all differ wildly in their understanding of Descartes, they also all agree on the huge significance and massive coherence of Cartesian thought. By contrast, Beckett's emphasis falls on Descartes's preference for omelettes made from eggs 'hatched from eight to ten days' (*cp*, p. 5). Consistency and 'linkage' are reduced to the level of a dottily fussy if not neurotic taste. Yet 'Whoroscope' is not just a *reductio ad absurdum* of the iron determination of the Cartesian project. 'The shuttle of a ripening egg combs the warp of his days', writes Beckett (ibid.): the hatching of the egg also becomes a metaphor for the development of Descartes' work and the progress of his life. But it remains an embryonic metaphor, even an 'abortion of a fledgling' (*cp*, p. 4). The poem has its 'granite point'. But it is a granite point of the granite point itself, a kind of degree zero of persistent will. Here as so often later, to adapt Heidegger, Beckett's concern was with the limit of something as where its life begins.

3

The Ruthless Cunning of the Sane:
London, 1933–5

Beckett returned from Paris to Dublin in September 1930, and started work as a Lecturer in French at Trinity College. In certain respects, it was rather as though he had returned to England. He told MacGreevy that suburban Foxrock was capable of inducing an 'ideally stupid' mood in which he would read 'the *Strand* magazine until it is time for tea and the *Illustrated Morning News* until it is time for bed'.[1] He felt more and more at odds with Englishness in Ireland. He found himself increasingly estranged from Rudmose-Brown and his Anglo-Irish preoccupations and manners, partly because of the fuss about *Le Kid*. He was equally estranged from the academic scene and his own genteel background. Here his mother played the hapless and unwitting role of cultural antagonist. This led to rows, in particular, one over a piece of his writing which clearly grated on her Protestant nerve-ends. The young Beckett's estrangement also expressed itself in a horror of his post. He repeatedly and famously said that 'he could not bear teaching to others what he did not know himself'.[2] This fastidious reluctance to dispense knowledge from on high had a historical dimension. What distressed Beckett was the assumption of the voice of Anglo-Irish superiority. Whilst Trinity still made it possible for him to speak in that voice, it was not one with which he felt able to identify.

This was by no means surprising. Ireland was moving in a direction that promised less and less scope to such voices. Between 1927 and 1932, two Irelands were locked in conflict, with one progressively superseding the other. Cosgrave and the 'Free Staters' were steadily losing power, whilst de Valera and Fianna Fáil were steadily gaining it. This meant a decisive shift towards a hardline Catholic, anti-British, agrarian nationalism. We get an exact sense of where this left Beckett if we compare his progress during these years to that of an older Anglo-Irish writer, W. B. Yeats. In the late 1920s, Yeats campaigned against the new legislation on censorship, divorce and the compulsory teaching of Gaelic. As Beckett's essay 'Censorship in the Saorstat' (1935) makes abundantly clear, his sympathies were with this party (which consisted very largely of 'a coterie of literary men').[3] The essay is withering about the Catholic Truth Society, the Irish as 'a characteristic agricultural community' and the pathetic

'Ireland governed by Catholic ideas alone': the Eucharistic Congress in O'Connell Street, Dublin, 1932.

'snuffles' of 'infant industries' in Ireland (*DI*, p. 86). The sardonic last reference is to nationalist hopes for serious industrial development. These had by then effectively been dashed.

After the 1932 elections, Ireland abolished the Anglo-Irish Treaty, gave itself a new constitution and cut all ties with the Commonwealth. In 1933, it abolished the Senate and the oath of allegiance. Thereafter, Yeats increasingly opposed 'an Ireland governed by Catholic ideas and Catholic ideas alone'.[4] Fearing for the place and role of Protestants in Ireland, he more and more withdrew his sympathies from Catholic nationalism. By 1934, however, he was also becoming anti-democratic and promoting a nostalgic concept of an aristocratic society governed by heroic figures. Beckett was not about to take this turn. In 'Recent Irish Poetry' (1934), whilst admitting that Yeats wove 'the best embroideries', he excoriated the 'leading [Celtic] twilighters' (*DI*, p. 71), their backward-looking antiquarianism and – derisively alluding to Yeats's 'Coole Park and Ballylee' – their production of 'segment after segment of cut-and-dried sanctity and loveliness' (ibid.).[5] He took issue with what he called 'the entire Celtic drill of extraversion' (*DI*, p. 73). Ireland had its scattered modern minds: MacGreevy, Denis Devlin, Brian Coffey. But the major cultural choices it offered were finally and equally cul-de-sacs.

Not surprisingly, therefore, in late 1931, Beckett gave up his post at Trinity. He fled to the Sinclairs in Germany, went back to Paris, lodged in the Gray's Inn Road in London, then returned to Dublin, where he was soon rowing with his mother again. His life during this time was indecisive, aimless and spotted with misery, tension and disaster. In December 1931, he crashed a car with Ethna MacCarthy on board, hurting her more than he did himself. In May 1933, Peggy Sinclair died. Then, in June 1933, so did his father. Beckett had loved his father, not least for his decency and warm-heartedness. His death snapped already fraying ties. Beckett soon decamped to London, where he lived from 1933 to 1935.

Beckett's London is a curious and striking thing. To some extent, as so often with writers and cities, one has to piece it together out of disparate bits. At the same time, it is important to draw out some of its more representative features. After 1922, southern Irish Protestants made up the great bulk of Irish emigrants. Irish Protestant culture had reached the end of a historical line. Protestants in Ireland now faced a dramatic loss of political and cultural power which spelt job discrimination and intolerance. Donald Akenson has shown that one-third of Southern Ireland's Protestant population left between 1911 and 1926.[6] Beckett grew up in an affluent but thinning Protestant suburb of Dublin. He could hardly have been unaware of the phenomenon of Protestant emigration. In 1933, he became part of the exodus specifically to Britain.

There was nothing at all strange about that. After 1922, Protestants were more likely to leave Ireland for Britain than anywhere else. Under the Anglo-Irish Treaty of 1921, the Irish retained their historical rights of free entry into the old colonial country without visa or work permit. Their destinations of choice, however, were no longer Scotland and the industrial north of England, as they had been in the nineteenth century, but one or other of the two locations in *Murphy*, London and the Home Counties. Not only were these the most affluent parts of England; the common perception of them was that they were bastions of conservative and middle-class English tradition, and were therefore the more likely to suit the refugees of a *colon* class. In the nineteenth century, Irish migrants to Britain had chiefly been poor and working-class. In the 1920s and '30s, by contrast, '"a better class of emigrant" became more visible',[7] an emigrant of higher social standing and educational level.

If, however, Irish Protestant migrants arrived in the host country with expectations deriving from their social and cultural status in Ireland, these expectations were likely to be more or less rudely disappointed. Irish Protestants had long identified with English culture in Ireland. But that hardly meant that English culture itself was likely to welcome them with open arms or as kindred spirits. Protestants arriving in England who regarded themselves as British on arrival discovered that they were, after all, very Irish. Furthermore, in England, anyone Irish was likely to be viewed through the lens of time-honoured stereotypes, and there was a pervasive and casual contempt for 'the Paddy'. According to Ultan Crowley, anti-Irish sentiment was particularly rife in England from 1922 to the 1940s, a legacy of the Anglo-Irish War and independence.[8] For the Irish, Protestants and Catholics alike, their identity became a problematic matter as soon as they opened their mouths, and no new English identity was readily available to them. Such attitudes did not distinguish between Protestants and Catholics: the English remained largely immune to any plea for differentiation. To them, the Irish were all Murphies: that may partly be why Beckett gives his very uncommon protagonist such a very common Irish Catholic name.[9]

Beckett shared both aspects of the Protestant migrant's experience of London. On the one hand, he had comparatively if modestly privileged connections. MacGreevy found a room for him in Paulton's Square, off the King's Road. This in itself is a less surprising setting for Beckett than it might seem: the 1931 census recorded heavy concentrations of Irish in Chelsea.[10] At the same time, he was not far away from a respectable if not distinguished social scene. MacGreevy himself, for example, was lodging just round the corner with Hester Dowden, daughter of Edward Dowden, one-time secretary of the Irish Liberal Union, vice-president of the Irish Unionist Alliance and, by the time of his death in 1913, the most eminent of all the literary professors at Trinity. Beckett occasionally played piano duets with Hester in Cheyne Walk Gardens, amidst the teacups, Pekinese dogs and Siamese cats. The image is worth pondering. Equally, he was in London partly to benefit from the new middle-class panacea, psychoanalysis, for which his mother was paying. His analyst was Wilfred Bion, another idiosyncratic and intellectually fascinating gentleman with a colonial background and a good English education – though Bion also had a distinguished war record. They met at the Tavistock clinic, then in cultivated Bloomsbury. Their relationship became friendly and informal, and they spent time in each other's company. Like Rudmose-Brown, Bion even had a nickname.

There was thus a sense in which Beckett's social environment in London was not very far removed from the one he had enjoyed (or failed to enjoy) in Dublin. Yet a great deal of his experience in London also pushed him closer to the typical predicament of the migrant. On his trip to London in 1932, for example, he had run up against the problem of finding rented accommodation in insalubrious parts of the city. This could be bewildering for Irish migrants, not least because furnished rooms were not a standard feature of Dublin life. To some extent, the Beckett of 1932 also shared the migrant's economic priorities and behaved accordingly, visiting agencies and, in his own phrase, 'creeping and crawling' for work with editors and publishers, notably resident Irishmen. He also repeatedly met with brusque rejection, or what he called 'glib cockney regrets'.[11]

If London seemed unamiable (as it had to Joyce),[12] Beckett responded in kind. He was unimpressed by historic London, finding the Tower uninteresting and the pompous nationalism of the interior of St Paul's hideous. He invested Pope's lines describing 'London's column' – the Monument, in Epistle III of the 'Moral Essays' – as a tall bully lifting its head with a significance Pope had not intended. It was not the only time Beckett would associate London with power and intimidation. He hated the city, particularly its pervasive and automatic racism, and the condescension routinely meted out to him as an Irishman.[13] Later in life, he called it 'Muttonfatville', and thought of it as singularly indifferent to human misery.[14] Not surprisingly, the London Irish tended to close in on themselves, to become small communities within the larger one. These communities defined themselves in isolation from the English around them. Beckett's friends in London, both male and female, were Irish.

As might be expected, in London Beckett was not only a solitary figure, but also given to nostalgia. He arrived in the metropolis in 1932, and quickly got involved in conversations about de Valera, who was in town at the same time.[15] Throughout 1934, Ireland remained the focus of much of Beckett's interest and attention.[16] This, too, was quite typical of Irish migrants to Britain. For reasons both geographic and historical, they did not see themselves as making the same kind of decisive break as migrants to the USA or Australasia. They were much more likely to move back and forth between source and host cultures, finding plenty of opportunities 'for continuing interactions with the homeland'.[17] The tendency to gravitate back to Ireland, in spirit if not in person, was only exacerbated by the graceless prejudices so frequently in evidence around them.

Return in mind as he might, however, Beckett was not inclined to do it decisively or fully. His analysis with Bion was gradually allowing him to detach himself from his mother, and all the issues that were at stake in his quarrels with her. Interestingly, when his mother arrived for a visit in 1935, he was able to give her something that suited her but was remote from his England, a motorized tour of 'pretty market-towns and cathedral cities'.[18] But the process (of detachment) was as yet incomplete. This is expressed in the circumstances of composition of Beckett's first major novel, *Murphy*. He began it in his lodgings in London, in August 1935. By Christmas of the same year, however, he was back in Dublin, where he caught pleurisy, was nursed by his mother and ended up fitting out a bedroom in Cooldrinagh as a study, in which he assembled his books from both Dublin and London and duly completed his novel.

If the Beckett of 1933 to 1935 remained suspended in a limbo that was cultural, intellectual and geographical all at once, this is exactly the condition dramatized in *Murphy* itself. It is an exercise in migrant writing. Murphy wants to be 'sovereign and free' (*MU*, p. 65), as did Ireland before 1922, though many Irish thought their country had properly been neither until 1933. Murphy, however, cannot identify with the versions of 'freedom' on offer in either Ireland or the Imperial capital. He therefore seeks his own peculiar form of Irish liberty 'in the dark, in the will-lessness, [as] a mote in its absolute freedom' (*MU*, p. 66). His pursuit of a distinctive freedom may ultimately be tragicomic. The novel nonetheless tells us a lot about what London meant to Beckett.

Murphy is a migrant. He has been in London for six or seven months, and Miss Counihan supposes him to be getting on with the migrant's task, 'sweating his soul out in the East End, so that I may have all the little luxuries to which I am accustomed' (*MU*, p. 126). All the considerations involved in Murphy's short-term future focus on London. Beckett endows him with some knowledge of Paris, but apparently not his own experience of having lived there. Murphy's Parisian references are to the right bank (the Gare St-Lazare, Rue d'Amsterdam and the Boulevard de Clichy) rather than Beckett's favourite *rive gauche*. The area around St-Lazare was even associated with London, not only because of the rail link, but via Huysmans, Mallarmé and Monet; though it seems probable that, given a taste which he shares with the Beckett of the period, Murphy is heading in the direction of the Place de Clichy for less cultivated reasons. As Henry Miller abundantly informs us, Clichy was well-known for its prostitutes.

Beckett also grants Murphy some of the reasons specifically for Protestant migration to England after 1922.[19] Like Beckett in 'Censorship in the Saorstaat', Murphy is repeatedly scathing about the 'new' Ireland. He shares Neary's dislike of falling 'among Gaels' (*MU*, p. 6). He is aided and abetted in his distaste by the novel itself,

Oliver Sheppard's 1911–12 statue of *The Death of Cuchulain* in the General Post Office, Dublin, 'Red Branch bum' invisible.

if in a succession of little touches, from the narrator's disparagement of the 'filthy censors' (*MU*, p. 47) and alleged Irish nepotism (*MU*, p. 95) to the fact that Ramaswami Suk's card distinguishes the Irish Free State from the Civilized World, to the image of Neary hilariously banging his head against Cuchulain's 'Red Branch bum' in the General Post Office. This last image, of course, desecrates not just republican and nationalist but equally Revivalist 'holy ground' (*MU*, p. 28, 30), fusing two objects of Beckettian distaste, as does taking the name of Cathleen ni Houlihan in vain (in the reference to Dublin waitress Cathleen na Hennessey). Revivalism again becomes the principal target in Murphy's memories of Irish writing as belches 'wet and foul from the green old days' (*MU*, p. 62), and his desire to have his ashes flushed down the lavatory at the Abbey Theatre, 'if possible during the performance of a piece' (*MU*, p. 151).

But if the novel makes Ireland seem backward and uninviting, it also makes London seem alienating. For Irish migrants, arriving in England spelled culture shock. London in particular was vast, its scale almost inconceivable to a Dubliner used to a manageable city that, in many ways, did not function or even look like a modern metropolis. From John O'Donoghue's *In A Strange Land* to Paddy Fahey's *The Irish in London* to Donal Foley's *Three Villages*, Irish migrant memoirs return to certain themes: amazement at the vastness of London, including its miles of indifferent housing; the speed of life, the predominance of clock time, the sense of time as a commodity, sharply divided between work and leisure; the lack of any feeling of immediate community; the simple absence of the colour green. Most of these themes appear in Beckett's novel, as in Murphy's reference to 'the sense of time as money . . . highly prized in business circles' (*MU*, p. 43), or his evocation of his 'medium-sized cage of north-western aspect commanding an unbroken view of medium-sized cages of south-eastern aspect' (*MU*, p. 5, 48). It is worth noting, too, that his 'mew' has been 'condemned' because it falls within a 'clearance area' (*MU*, p. 5, 15), reflecting the patterns of rapid construction and destruction of housing in the London of the period. This was yet another source of bewilderment to the migrant, whose disorientation was intensified by the sense that the metropolis was not only a Leviathan, but a protean one. It is therefore not surprising that the novel as a whole should have its occasional strains of pastoral wistfulness, as in Celia's feeling for an Irish sky that is 'cool, bright, full of movement' and 'anoint[s] the eyes' (*MU*, p. 27).

Life in England was not invariably unrewarding. Murphy himself finds certain liberations in the migrant experience. Nonetheless, for the Irish migrant, the encounter with the host culture was likely to be problematic if not traumatic. Beckett's novel underlines Murphy's difficulty with questions of his position. In fact, independent Irishmen promptly lost their independent political status in England, since, in British eyes at least, Irish citizens were still viewed 'as subjects'.[20] At the level of daily life, this attitude was reproduced as the racism I noted earlier. Murphy runs right up against it, notably in the scene with the chandlers on the Gray's Inn Road, where he is derided as not looking 'rightly human', that is, jeered at as the familiar type of the anthropoid Irishman from whom he has earlier sought to distinguish himself (*MU*, p. 47).

If Beckett gives him some of the migrant's reasons for being in England, however, Murphy also stoutly resists the migrant's logic. He is indifferent to Miss Counihan's agenda. He plays the role of migrant with a mixture of intellectual *bouffonnerie* and ironical *désinvolture*, and thereby struggles to rise superior to its tribulations, oppressions and disempowerments. Indeed, in many ways, he is not only an untypical but an antitypical migrant. For he rejects the migrant's internalized self-image, the former colonizer's conception of the migrant as an eminently usable resource. He ostentatiously resists some of the preoccupations in the surrounding national culture, conceptions of life that the good, obedient migrant labourer was supposedly the better for absorbing. This is notably the case with health and diet. In 1930s England, health was becoming something of a national fixation. It even became an election issue. Every popular magazine had its regular feature on health. This was by no means simply a concern of the right's. On the left, too, 'there was a whole literature on nutrition, on the class-incidence of health'.[21] Behind all this, of course, was an uneasy awareness that Germany was massively training young Germans in physical fitness: hence the British Physical Fitness Bill

'British Physical Fitness': the 'Festival of Youth' in Wembley Stadium, London, 1937.

of 1936. Murphy, however, is categorically indifferent to this drive, and it is an object of parody in the well-known account of his lunch: 'Murphy's fourpenny lunch was a ritual vitiated by no base thoughts of nutrition. . . . "A cup of tea and a packet of assorted biscuits." Twopence the tea, twopence the biscuits, a perfectly balanced meal' (*MU*, p. 49).

Murphy also repudiates the Irish migrants' habit of sticking together on the one hand, and oscillating between England and Ireland on the other. Wylie, Miss Counihan and Cooper both lead an existence split between Ireland and England, and cling together as a self-contained group. By contrast, Murphy has no interest at all in any expatriate Irish community and does not shuttle back and forth between cultures. Beckett's ironical migrant novel even rethinks the geography of the imperial capital and redefines its spaces. In effect, it resists an official topography. Take Lincoln's Inn Fields, for example. The London County Council had acquired it in 1895, and opened it up to the public. Lutyens had recently remodelled its most eminent building, Newcastle House. Murphy, however, strips it of its new appearance of modern benignity and reawakens its historical identity, a world of cozeners and cozened, of 'crossbiting and conycatching and sacking and figging', of 'pillory and gallows' (*MU*, p. 48).

This is very much in line with Beckett's overriding conception of the brutality and rapacity of London. For in a novel which ends with the hero dying in a lunatic asylum, London is a city dominated by 'the ruthless cunning of the sane' (*MU*, p. 50). This was clearly how Beckett saw it. Lois Gordon emphasizes the importance of the effects of the Depression on the Britain that Beckett encountered when he arrived, in 1933.[22] But Beckett's England is hardly that of the Jarrow march. Indeed, there is no sense at all in *Murphy* of the politics of London in the 1930s, its strongly Labour culture, its Fascists and their attacks on Jews, its Communist groups, its conspicuous Left intellectuals.[23] The Beckett of *Murphy* may seem strikingly melancholic. But he shares none of the specific melancholy that animates, say, the W. H. Auden of *Look, Stranger* (1936), with its haunting awareness of imminent historical catastrophe. In the 1930s, even the British Conservative Prime Minister-to-be Harold Macmillan thought that 'the structure of capitalist society in its old form had broken down'.[24] This does not appear to have occurred to Beckett. Indeed, he seems to present us with a very different if not actually opposed perception of economic circumstances.

However, by the years during which Beckett was actually living in London, 1933–5, the British economy was to some extent recovering from the Depression and even experiencing a mini-boom. No doubt this was little felt in Jarrow. But London and the Home Counties were particularly undepressed. London supported 'the country's most affluent community' and was 'confident and expanding' as never before, offering a dazzling choice of occupations and pastimes.[25] It remained the financial capital of the world. This is the London Beckett sees; in other words, he sees the Imperial capital from the point of view of a colonial migrant.

London is a 'mercantile gehenna' (*MU*, p. 26), the wealthy metro-
politan centre of an imperial economic power. Its law is that of the
'*Quid pro quo!*' (*MU*, p. 5), the law of exchange, the market. Nor is
'the ruthless cunning of the sane' merely that of the plutomaniacs
against whose deadly weaponry a 'seedy solipsist' is doomed to
pit himself in vain (*MU*, p. 50). The primacy of cunning in the metropolis appears repeatedly in social relations both significant and
trivial. Whether with Miss Carridge and her preoccupation with
'domestic economy' (*MU*, p. 43), the chandlers, Vera the waitress or
Rosie Dew, again and again, Murphy's relationships are repeatedly
inflected by commerce and the economic interests of others.

This is above all what is at stake in his relationship with Celia.
The issue on which the whole novel in fact hinges is whether, by
insisting on the laws of exchange – love for financial security – Celia
can convert the ironical migrant Murphy to the economism of the
host country and the economic logic of the typical Irish migrant.
Of course, she fails. Murphy is very interested in making love in
England – his principal experience of migration as liberating – but
remains entirely uninterested in making money there. True, this
is not altogether remote from Irish migrant experience: one of the
worries, for the Irish back home and, above all, the Irish Catholic
church, was that Irishmen and women were likely to become much
more relaxed about sexual morality as a result of living in decadent,
modern, materialist England. At the same time, if the rot did set in,
it was hardly as the result of a bohemian rejection of economic considerations. Its breeding-ground was much more likely to be (for
example) the Irish dance-halls, to which hard-working Irish people
in England increasingly turned for entertainment, companionship
and consolation.

But Murphy unrelentingly refuses to adopt the economic
rationale of the Irish migrant. His mind is never 'on the correct
cash-register lines' (*MU*, p. 101). Perhaps his most crucial form
of resistance lies in his struggle to overturn the structure of the

English morality of work. Here, again, Murphy confronts and challenges stereotypes. English employers often thought of Irish employees as unusually hardworking. There were obvious reasons for this: economic migrancy meant that diligence was at a premium. Since migrant workers were frequently sending money home, it made sense for them to show an unusual degree of commitment to their jobs. Yet, contradictorily, some of the dominant English stereotypes were also of the Irish as slovenly and indolent. Even J. B. Priestley, writing in the 1930s, presented the Irish as not given to effort and natural slum-dwellers.[26] Beckett and Murphy do not seek to challenge this stereotype. They rather seek to overturn the system of value that subtends both it and the English valuation of the industrious migrant labourer. It is not work, but indolence, the avoidance of work, that Murphy turns into an almost philosophical principle. In so doing, again, he challenges both the triumphant mercantilism of the old colonial power and the economic logic of Irish migration.

Finally, *Murphy* also redefines another important aspect of the Irish migrant's historical experience: his or her relationship to the British asylum. For Irish migrants, life in England could also mean psychological distress. The admission rates of Irish-born patients into English asylums were exceptionally high. Liam Greenslade suggests that this was due to the problem of objecti-fication within the host culture. Since his national identity became a problematic object of attention as soon as he spoke, but no new English identity was immediately available to him, the Irish migrant endured a 'pathological double-bind' which prevented the formation of 'a stable cultural identity'.[27] For the most part, he was condemned to internalize the pathological projection of the colonizer, and therefore to be always at odds with his own image.

Murphy emphatically repudiates this projection. Irish patients in asylums had usually been working-class and Catholic, whilst the medical staff were predominantly English, middle-class and

Protestant.[28] Murphy goes voluntarily into an asylum, but on the side of the dominant power. He even refers to the inmates as another 'race' (*MU*, p. 97). Yet at the same time, he identifies with them and wishes to learn from them. He thus radically dissociates himself from the common position of the Irish migrant within the asylum, whilst also climbing down from his own relatively superior position. In the end, however, his efforts fail him. He seeks to subvert and ironize the role of the migrant from a migrant position. But the ironical space into which he moves finally turns out to be a dead-end. The experience of the ironical or antitypical migrant is just like the experience of the typical one, in being, in the end, an experience of definitive failure and loss.

Interestingly, in the years 1932–8, for Irishmen and women, the Depression was not in fact the principal economic concern. They were more preoccupied with the so-called Anglo-Irish 'economic war'. This began with a British imposition of an import tax on Irish goods. De Valera and Fianna Fáil saw it as an attempt to browbeat Ireland on the Anglo-Irish Treaty by other than military or political means. It endangered the cause of Irish freedom, and had to be resisted at all costs. So Ireland imposed its own duties in turn. It claimed to be aspiring to (a Murphy-like) self-sufficiency. This cost it very dearly, where the British imposition cost Britain little or nothing. Indeed, Sean Lemass, Minister for Industry and Commerce, feared the return of famine conditions in Ireland.[29] De Valera remained resolute, however, telling Ireland that it must accept deprivation as its lot if necessary, shoulder the burden of poverty, and agree to a diet of 'frugal fare'.[30]

There is a sense in which one might think of Murphy as conducting his own private version of an economic war with England, on de Valera's terms. Furthermore, he does so on the basis of unworldly terms that sound very Beckettian, but are also strikingly close to de Valera's, not least in that Murphy accepts that 'frugal fare' is the necessary consequence of the struggle. By a strange and wonderfully paradoxical logic so characteristic of Beckett, the antitypical, deeply ironical migrant apparently so disdainful of Ireland, Irish independence and the Irish is finally identifiable, not only with the Irish migrant per se, but with the historical cause of Ireland itself.

Here we can finally come back to Yeats. If, in the 1930s, Yeats became ever more distant from Catholic Ireland, this did not mean that he gave up on his own nationalism or its anti-Imperial and anti-British dimensions. He remained proud of the Irish fight for freedom, not least what it achieved by means of the Statute of Westminster in 1931, which granted Ireland legislative sovereignty, and finally allowed it to declare itself a fully-fledged republic. He continued to attack British imperialist politics in the 1930s and was still inclined to see English culture as plagued by racism, hypocrisy, materialism and blind economism. 'I hate certain characteristics of modern England', he wrote.[31] Beckett would have said the same. For all its paradoxical identification with Ireland, however, *Murphy* also remains marooned between two finally unacceptable cultures, just as Yeats was in old age, and Beckett was between 1933 and 1935. It soon became clear, however, that in Beckett's case, unlike Yeats's, other options were available.

4

Melancholia *im dritten Reich*: Germany, 1936–7

By late 1936, it seemed as though Beckett's limbo might swallow him up. He had completed *Murphy*, but both Chatto & Windus and Heinemann had quickly rejected it. He was thirty, and his mother was nagging him about his future career. He considered taking up menial employment in the family business, which his brother Frank was now running, and indulged in one or two extravagantly unrealistic fantasies, writing to Eisenstein to ask whether he might not train with him at the State Institute of Cinematography in Moscow, and even entertaining the bizarre idea of becoming an aviator. At the same time, when, by a piece of mild good fortune, he was offered the editorship of the *Dublin Magazine*, he turned it down, though he seemed well suited to it. He had a brief affair with an old childhood friend, Mary Manning, now married and Boston-based. By the time she went back home, he himself had decided to run from his predicament, leaving Dublin for Germany.

Beckett was by no means unfamiliar with German culture and the German language, not least because of his relationship with Peggy Sinclair. In 1928, he had travelled to Laxenburg, just south of Vienna, where Peggy was taking a course, and spent several weeks there. Whilst prosecuting their affair in 1928–9, he had also made several trips to Kassel, where the Sinclairs lived. Though he and Peggy had broken up, he had returned to see the Sinclairs in Kassel at Christmas in 1931, after his abrupt departure from Trinity College. All this had left its mark on *Dream of Fair to Middling Women*, which has claims to being Beckett's most Germanic literary work. Plentiful 'scraps of German' – and of Germany – were clearly already 'play[ing] in his mind' (*DFMW*, p. 191). In 1936, however, instead of central Hesse, for the first time, Beckett headed for northern Germany, where he knew no one. He started in Hamburg on 2 October 1936. In the long run, the trip would take in Lubeck, Luneburg, Hanover, Brunswick, Hildesheim, Berlin, Halle, Weimar, Erfurt, Naumburg, Leipzig, Dresden, Pillnitz, Meissen, Freiberg, Bamberg, Wurzburg, Nuremberg, Regensburg and Munich. He also kept a diary.

By 1936, Germany had transformed itself. Hitler and the Nationalsozialistische Deutsche Arbeiterpartei (the NSDAP or Nazi party) had been in power since 1933. They had immediately introduced press censorship and suspended civil liberties. By the end of the year, they had opened the first concentration camp at

Police round up Communists and undesirable aliens in a Jewish quarter of Berlin in the early days of Nazi rule, 1933.

Dachau, dissolved the labour unions and organized public burnings of un-German books. The new Germany was stridently aggressive. To many, it was clear in which direction events were leading. In 1935, Erich Ludendorff, former chief of German staff, ex-member of the Reichstag and one-time Hitler ally, turned Clausewitz on his head in *Total War*. The same year saw Germany walk out of the League of Nations and the Disarmament Conference and introduce universal military training, in defiance of the Treaty of Versailles. The drives at stake were inexorable. In the first instance, they were leading towards *Kristallnacht*, the *Anschluss* and the German entry into the Sudetenland, all of which took place in 1938. Beckett was certainly aware of them.

The order of the day was *Gleichshaltung*: everyone had to 'fall into line'. Germany was caught up in an immense drive to uniformity, and turned punitively on citizens deemed to be racially, mentally or physically defective. The NSDAP brought in a Sterilization Law for the disabled as early as 1933, and founded the Racial Policy Office in 1934. On 15 September 1935, it introduced the Nuremberg Laws. The first law, the Law for the Protection of German Blood and German Honour, prohibited marriages and extramarital sex between Germans and Jews, whilst the second, the Reich Citizenship Law, stripped persons not considered of German blood of their German citizenship. In any case, from 1933 onwards, the Nazis had been eliminating the left-wing press and steadily purging Jews, Communists and sometimes liberal opponents from the civil service, medical profession, universities, municipal authorities, churches and other professional, social and cultural organizations. Most ominously of all, by 1936, head of the SS Heinrich Himmler had full control of all German police.

Deirdre Bair suggests that Beckett's encounter with Nazi Germany came as a shock to him. But he was not ignorant of the political situation.[1] The diaries repeatedly indicate that he was either wearily familiar with Nazism beforehand, or very rapidly became so.[2] He had no doubt learnt a lot from his earlier experience of Germany; from the Sinclairs themselves, who had returned to Ireland, partly because of William Sinclair's Jewishness; and from newspapers, of which he was an avid reader. He got the *Irish Times* regularly from home, and read a number of different German newspapers and magazines – the *Reichszeitung der Deutschen Erzieher, Frankfurter Zeitung, Hamburger Tageblatt, Berliner Tageblatt, Lustige Blätter, Dresdner Nachrichten, Leipziger Nachrichten, Dresdner Anzeiger, Bamberger Volksblatt* and even the Nazi *Volkischer Beobachter* – at different times. Certainly, by late February 1937, he was stressing how often he had heard the Party line (*GD*, 24.2.37).

Nor did Beckett exactly 'withdraw' from what he saw of a monstrous society into art,[3] though he certainly spent a very great deal of his trip steeping himself in painting and literature. At the same time, he emphatically declared his lack of interest in an art of explicit social or political criticism (*GD*, 28.12.36). To intellectuals hungry for a meditated Beckettian dissection of contemporary Germany, the diaries may seem frustrating. Beckett seldom comments at any length on the German scene.[4] But anyone hopeful of finding an aesthetics thoughtfully and coherently elaborated in reaction to Germany will also be a little disappointed.[5] The commentaries and theses on art and literature in the diaries appear here and there, in sporadic and disjointed fashion. The diaries themselves are concerned with a more particular and in some degree obscure experience than such terms suggest. Beckett's responses to Nazi Germany were quite often visceral as much as intellectual, and frequently turbulent and intense, if in some ways contained.

Very occasionally, Beckett adopted some rather odd ideas about Germany. He agreed with Axel Kaun, for example, that Goebbels was really the malign genius of the *Bewegung* (the 'Movement'), whilst Hitler and Goering were sentimentalists (*GD*, 19.1.37). But he was not at all 'confused' by Germany.[6] He was hardly stupid. He was extremely conscious of the new German *Lebensanschauung* (view of life). He encountered it routinely: in waiters' talk, for example (*GD*, 24.1.37, 28.1.37). He took the pulse of the new Germany through details. He was sensitive, for instance, to some of the more crassly masculine forms of the new culture: SA brass bands (*GD*, 14.2.37), groups of soldiers in public houses and churches (*GD*, 22.2.37, 4.3.37). He heard endless repetitions of the *Hitlergruss* (*Heil Hitler!*) in a *Bierstube* (*GD*, 5.12.36) and elsewhere. He listened to the carousings of the *Hitlerjugend*, just three weeks after membership of the organization had been made compulsory for all young German men (*GD*, 24.1.37).

He was not only aware of the general temper of what was going on in Germany. He knew or learnt a great deal about its particularities. He immediately understood that Germany was intent on war. He intuited this very soon after his arrival from a radio broadcast of Hitler and Goebbels haranguing the crowd at the inauguration of the *Winterhilfswerk* (*GD*, 6.10.36).[7] The certainty of oncoming war hangs over the diaries like a pall: Beckett speculates, for example, on how war would be likely to affect a fellow-lodger in Hamburg (*GD*, 17.10.36). The goal of the Four-Year Plan, which was introduced at the annual NSDAP rally in 1936, and about which Beckett twice heard Hitler and Goering speaking on the radio (*GD*, 28.10.36, 30.1.37), was to prepare the German army and economy for war within a few years. The menace of Soviet Communism was the pretext for German rearmament. Beckett's diaries note that Russian troops are supposedly massing on the Polish border (*GD*, 16.11.36) and remark, with varying degrees of irony, on the 'threat from Moscow' and film about it (*GD*, 11.10.36), and attacks on the Moscow *'Judenklique'* (*GD*, 24.10.36). They also comment disapprovingly on anti-Bolshevist propaganda (*GD*, 1.11.36) and anti-Russian sentiments (*GD*, 7.11.36). Beckett even humorously claims to be keeping a list of items under the rubric '*Moskau droht*' ('Moscow is threatening', *GD*, 1.11.36). In the *Frankfurter Zeitung*, he later read a justification of war as a catalytic accelerator of the historical process (*GD*, 14.3.37). That Germany signed the anti-Comintern Pact with Japan on 25 November – as Beckett knew from hearing Goebbels broadcasting on the subject on the radio (*GD*, 25.11.36) – must have made the 'acceleration' seem all the nearer.

Hitler had recently declared that the Germans required *Lebensraum*, more space, more sources of food and raw materials, and were aiming at *Autarkie*, economic self-sufficiency. Beckett heard some of the standard arguments for both: Germany lacked colonies, particularly after the Treaty of Versailles, as the other major European powers did not, and so could not feed its population; Germany needed to do without imports and establish a national currency independent of foreign ones (*GD*, 17.10.36). VoMi, the *Volksdeutsche Mittelstelle*, was founded in 1936 to coordinate policies towards German minorities outside Germany. Hitler had expanded the Weimar Republic's definition of the *Volksdeutsche* to include German citizens of other countries as well as German residents in them. This would soon become a principal justification for invasions to the East. Beckett was aware of the theme, notably with regard to the racial composition of Czechoslovakia (*GD*, 19.1.37, 7.3.37).

Within three days of arriving in Hamburg, he was commenting ruefully on the Nazi purges of inconveniently nondescript humanity. Not a whore to be found on the Reeperbahn, he noted: they seemed to have been all locked up (*GD*, 5.10.36). The NSDAP had been interning 'asocials' or *Gemeinschaftsunfähigen*, those unfit for society, since 1933. They included beggars, vagrants, alcoholics and prostitutes. In 1936, they were particularly embarrassing. For 1936 saw that peculiarly grandiose celebration of *Fähigkeit* (capability), the Berlin Olympic Games. These ended just six weeks before Beckett arrived; he was unremittingly scornful of the values they represented, preferring 'the fundamental unheroic'.[8] His work would later defend and even revel in *Unfähigkeit*. The concept became key to his aesthetics, as for example in the famous discussion of 'inability', not being able, in *Three Dialogues* (*DI*, p. 145). The roots of Beckett's feeling for incapacity were doubtless elsewhere. Nonetheless, his experience of Germany in 1936–7 clearly provided a vital additional reason for his identification with hapless outsiders. Of the painters of the Hamburg Sezession, in whom he had a 'special interest' and whom he took to be 'alert witnesses of Germany in 1936',[9] he was particularly drawn to Willem Grimm, because, in 1936, he appeared to be attracting so much personal abuse, and seemed *verbummelt*, dissolute, a man who was down on his luck (*GD*, 24–25.11.36).

Beckett knew about Nazi racial policies well before he reached Germany. It is clear from the diaries that, in Germany itself, he came to know about them in some detail. In 1933, Alfred Rosenberg had taken the Nordische Gesellschaft – the organization for German-Nordic cooperation – under Nazi protection, increasingly sweeping the Nordic peoples into a 'greater German Reich'.[10] On 13 September 1936, the NSDAP had announced the foundation of the *Lebensborn* agency to encourage young unmarried women to give birth to Nordic children. As George Orwell indicated on 17 October, by this time, the word 'Nordic' had a singular charge.[11] Beckett's dispassionate response, just ten days later, to a group of German-speaking Scandinavians at the Nordische Gesellschaft in Hamburg suggests a conscious distaste for the doctrine of Nordic racial superiority (*GD*, 27.10.36).

Above all, Beckett was extremely aware of the persecution of German Jews. He notes, for example, that art-historian Rosa Schapire could not publish or give public lectures because she was not of pure Aryan descent (*GD*, 15.11.36). He discovered that Gretchen Wohlwill, the Jewish 'Mother' of the Hamburg Sezession, was now regarded as an unsuitable custodian of German culture (*GD*, 21.11.36).[12] He listened to stories about Jews (*GD*, 23.2.37) and ferocious anti-Semitic diatribes (*GD*, 22.2.37), heard Jews blamed for problems in trade (*GD*, 28.1.37), and saw photographers outside Jewish shops and ugly anti-Semitic slogans on walls (GD, 21.1.37, 16.2.37). Acquaintances openly expressed their hatred of Jews. In Berlin, for example, his landlord Kempt told him the history of his own personal anti-Semitism (GD, 6.1.37). Beckett knew the term *Rassenschande*, racial disgrace, knew what it meant in Hitler's Germany – sex between Jews and non-Jews – and knew that the first Nuremberg Law forbade that non-Aryan households employ Aryan women under 45, for fear of it (GD, 24.11.36). The corollaries to the Reich Citizen Act of 14 November 1936 defined categories of *Mischlinge*, racial mixtures, and Beckett was aware of the issue of racial exclusivity and arguments made for it (GD, 29.3.37).

His responses to the monstrosities of Nazi Germany are various. For about two months, he thought of writing a work that might be ruefully appropriate to the Third Reich, what he referred to as his *Journal of a Melancholic* (GD, 31.10.36). No such work appears to have survived,[13] but Beckett might have given the title to the diaries themselves. They are nothing if not a tale of protracted melancholy, as he himself was aware (GD, 18.10.36). Indeed, they are at times devoured by what Evelyne Grossman describes as a Beckettian 'passion mélancolique'.[14] As at other times in his life, however, Beckett's melancholy did not preclude resistance. Indeed, the two went hand in hand. He illegally acquired Max Sauerlandt's banned account of the art of the preceding thirty years. He got hold of Karl Heinemann's German literary history precisely because it had appeared before the *Machtübernahme* (Nazi takeover).[15] He was stiffly dismissive of historical narratives of the German nation (GD, 15.1.37). He was profoundly suspicious of anyone who appeared even faintly to believe in the *Sonderweg*, the special German way (ibid.). He was repelled by any conception of the uniqueness of the German *Schicksal* or fate, indeed, by German narratives as and of heroic journeys in general. This he made clear to Kaun on 15 January 1937:

I say I am not interested in a 'unification' of the historical chaos any more than I am in the 'clarification' of the individual chaos, + still less in the anthropomorphisation of the inhuman necessities that provoke the chaos. What I want is the straws, flotsam, etc., names, dates, births & deaths, because that is all I can know.[16]

Not the wave, but the corks upon it: after all, as he adds, drily, later in the diaries (*GD*, 20.1.37), the twentieth is the century of God's *aboulia*, a pathological failure of divine will and powers of decisive action.

If the young Beckett's nature included any will seriously to conform to iron norms, it was at best exiguous. He was ill-adapted to the culture of *Gleichshaltung*, and temperamentally at odds with it.[17] This made for irreverence and disrespect. He suggested, for example, that the Nazis might create a cadre of HH, *Hitlerhuren*, Hitler Whores, to match the SS (*GD*, 6.2.37). He referred to *Mein Kampf* as *Sein Krampf*, and the *Vierjahresplan* as the *Bierjahresplan*.[18] When he went to a talk by Werner Lorenz, SS Gruppen- and shortly to be Obergruppenführer, General of the Waffen-SS and police and, from January 1937, chief of VoMi, he gave the fascist salute with the wrong arm (*GD*, 11.10.36). The fact that he describes himself as partly saluting Horst Wessel makes it the more piquant. Wessel was the official martyr of the Nazi movement (killed by Communists after a dispute with his landlady). The Horst Wessel song had been the Nazi anthem since 1931. Wessel's name had recently been in the news, because Hitler had commissioned the ship that bore it as a *Schulschiff*.[19] Beckett clearly felt a particular distaste for Wessel (a maniacally violent creature, whose animality he deftly indicates, *GD*, 19.12.36). He remarks in Berlin that, ironically enough, Wessel was raised in Judenstrasse (*GD*, 18.12.36).

Beckett could not be wooed: urged by Claudia Asher – apparently Nazi-inclined and anti-Semitic[20] – to surrender his *Abstand* (detachment) for the *Abgrund* (abyss), he doggedly replied that he intended to buy the complete works of Schopenhauer (*GD*, 24.10.36). He knew of the Nazi *Kraft durch Freude* division, which organized cultural and leisure activities for the working classes, and stated that he preferred his own KDF, Kaspar [sic] David Friedrich (*GD*, 1.11.36, 9.2.37; German graffiti artists still play with the initials today).[21] He wilfully refused to associate the *Verfassung der Ehe* (marriage bond) with anything more than sex (*GD*, 1.11.36), which takes on a particular significance in the light of the Nuremberg Laws. In 1933, Hitler had declared Munich to be 'the city of German art'.[22] Beckett views fascist architecture like Paul Ludwig Troost's monumental new Haus der deutschen Kunst in Munich with scrupulous disfavour. It lacks imagination, he declares, and smells of *Furcht vor Schmuck*, fear of ornament (*GD*, 10.3.37).

Otherwise, firstly: he walks. David Addyman has recently brilliantly argued that Beckett's work is characterized both by its topophobia, its resistance to all thought of 'emplacement', and a sober recognition that one is never truly out of place.[23] This might be the case with much of it. But it isn't really the case with the *German Diaries*. In the Hamburg section in particular, but also elsewhere, Beckett is intent on noting down street names, place-names, names of buildings, usually without further comment. He tells us where he went, where he went next, where he went after that . . . One explanation, clearly, is that, *contra* Addyman in this case, he is concerned to feel at home in a new town.[24] But this is to forget an obvious precursor. Beckett's assemblages of names recall Joyce's. Joyce, of course, famously declared that if Dublin were destroyed it could be rebuilt with *Ulysses* as guide. His art was, in this respect, a work of conservation or memorialization. So, too, in a world where, as he already knew, Hitler and Goebbels were heading for war, haphazardly, without Joyce's sense of coherent purpose, Beckett recorded places simply as *having been there*.

Secondly: he talks. From the start of his trip, he showed himself to be quite unusually avid for conversation with comparative strangers. He was determined to find useful German conversation partners (*GD*, 13.10.36), paying for language with beer if necessary (*GD*, 2.11.36). But the German that Beckett heard in conversation was a particular German. Early on in the diaries, he speculated on the German translation of 'bilge' (a word he used in connection with Smyllie and Oliver St John Gogarty among others, *GD*, 1.11.36, 7.1.37). He quickly recalled one: *Quatsch*.[25] It recurs throughout the diaries. He increasingly heard ordinary Germans' 'emissions' (*GD*, 22.11.36) as a discourse, or a set of related discourses. These discourses were stuffed with contemporary German notions: the *Führer*, the *Bewegung, Rassenschande, Blut und Boden* (blood and soil). Furthermore, apparently more neutral words – *Energie, Wollen* (will), *Ehre* (honour), *Helden* (heroes), *Verhetzung* (instigation), *Schwärmerei* (enthusiasm), *Reinheit* (purity) – had taken on disquieting new implications.

Beckett genuinely listened to Nazi Germany. He listened attentively.[26] He was acutely conscious of voices and what they could tell him about his circumstances. In Berlin, for example, he heard Kempt's and others' adoration of Hitler in their voices (*GD*, 19.1.37, 5.3.37). Individuals repeatedly spoke fervently of the *Bewegung*. He heard the effects of propaganda in others' voices, whether it was for the new autobahns or the wonders of the Schorfheide (*GD*, 5.1.37; Goering owned a mansion there, and planned to establish it as a National Socialist nature reserve). But he also heard equivocation. Whilst the mass of German people had rallied behind Hitler well before 1936 – on 29 March of that year, 99 per cent of Germans voted for the Nazis – in practice, many people compromised, colluded, practised doublethink, adopted the role of the *Mitläufer* or fellow traveller. The historian Pierre Ayçoberry describes this as the period in which the German middle classes in particular took 'Continue to function' as their maxim.[27] Beckett's German milieu tended to be fairly bourgeois and respectable, notably in Hamburg, and, however fitfully, he was aware that others were sometimes playing a double game.

His response to this doubleness is striking. He repeatedly distinguishes people from their historically and culturally determined language, the discourses of the day in which they are caught up. Thus talking to a man called Power prompts him to observe that people's relative likeability and the views they hold frequently have little to do with each other (*GD*, 16.11.36). Here and there, he adopts a practice of double notation. The *Wirt* he encounters at a *Gasthaus* on 16 February 1937, for example, spouts the usual rubbish; but he is also, Beckett adds, a nice man and a faintly touching figure. Ida Bienert recites the Nazi litany but is very amiable (*GD*, 11.2.37, 15.2.37). Decent individuals take up appalling positions (*GD*, 20.12.36). Of course, it is hard to know just where this kind of perception tips over into irony; part of what Beckett saw very clearly in Germany is that niceness does not save nice people from complicity. On the contrary: it may be precisely a conviction of the one that protects them from a consciousness of the other. But he certainly exercised, and would continue to exercise, a fine capacity for distinguishing between individuals and their platitudes or *Quatsch*.

Hence, as far as talking German is concerned, a different Beckettian project emerges in the shadow of the autodidactic one, a characteristically ironical project. However 'absurd and inconsequential' the logic, Beckett remarks that his drive to master another language is in fact a struggle 'to be master of another silence'.[28] Learning a language that he encountered in a historically specific and deeply rebarbative manifestation gave fresh impetus to his emerging concept of an art that might redeem the silence beyond language, not least, because, at a time when language is afflicted with historical disaster, silence must guard the principle of its possible renewal. Already, in *Dream of Fair to Middling Women*, he had written of Beethoven's 'vespertine compositions eaten away with terrible silences', and of his music as a whole as 'pitted with dire stroms of silence' (*DFMW*, pp. 138–39). On 9 July 1937, not long after leaving Germany, Beckett wrote a famous German letter to Kaun which protests against the 'terrible materiality of the word surface' (*DI*, p. 172), and asks whether it cannot be dissolved into silence, 'like for instance the sound surface, torn by enormous pauses, of Beethoven's Seventh Symphony' (ibid.).

Thirdly: he immerses himself in art. Once again, however, those who approach the diaries expecting a sumptuous feast of criticism may possibly feel a bit cheated. In late 1936, Goebbels had declared the end of art criticism. Since the NSDAP was going to see to it that only good German art was displayed, there was no need for critics any longer. If he was aware of Goebbels' directive, however, Beckett shows little inclination to resist it very spiritedly. The diaries include a few exquisite comments on individual works of art, notably regarding three great paintings, Giorgione's *Self-portrait*, which Beckett saw in Brunswick, and Antonello da Messina's *St Sebastian* and Vermeer's *The Procuress*, which he saw in Dresden. Quite often, however, the moments of appreciation amount merely to brief expressions of taste. When Beckett likes paintings, he may note that they are marvellous, wonderful, magnificent, charming or lovely. He gives reasons for doing so only comparatively seldom.

But the reasons of course are self-evident. In Nazi Germany, loveliness was uniquely threatened. Beckett refused to accept the priorities that were making that possible, and the consequences of which he was hearing all around him. He brusquely dismissed both the Nazi taste in kitsch and art that stank of National Socialist propaganda (*GD*, 6.1.36, 4.1.37, 19.3.37). The day after an interminable harangue from Kempt on the Beer Hall putsch (1923) and the Night of the Long Knives (1934), he promptly sought refuge in the Kronprinzenpalais and bathed himself in De Chirico, Modigliani, Kokoschka, Feininger, Munch and Van Gogh. This was typical: he scathingly dismissed all talk of 'politics' (by which he meant Nazi talk), and concentrated on museums and paintings with a dedication which would seem almost obsessive, were it not so clearly an act of defiance.

This was particularly the case with modern art. From 1933, Alfred Rosenberg's *NS-Kulturgemeinde* (National Socialist Cultural Community) and Goebbels' rival Culture Chamber (the *Reichs-kulturkammer)* increasingly controlled art and culture in Germany.[29] (Beckett heard others accuse Rosenberg, quite rightly, of being the principal foe of modern art in Germany, *GD*, 23.11.36). The new institutions proclaimed a new German art, and waged war on modernism. Beckett arrived in Germany at the end of a three-year period in which the Nazis had progressed from marginalizing modern art to banning it. The NSDAP increasingly instructed painters as to what, how much and where they could exhibit. Finally, on 5 November 1936, it ordered gallery directors to remove examples of decadent modern art from their walls. The purge would reach its climax in Munich in July 1937, with the Great German Art Exhibition on the one hand and the Degenerate Art show on the other.

Beckett was extremely conscious of how painters and paintings were affected by Nazi proscriptions. He knew very well, for example, how far, from 1933, the *Machtübernahme* had affected the painters of the Hamburg Sezession. Their working conditions had deterio-rated, and opportunities for showing their work had dwindled. Some of them had been intimidated and denounced. Beckett specifically grasped the 'inconsequence' of National Socialist cultural politics, the result, not least, of disagreements between Goebbels and Rosenberg as to what actually constituted degenerate art.[30] He found modern paintings still on display in some locations, in others not. He knew that certain museum catalogues had suddenly become inaccurate (*GD*, 30.10.36). He knew of painters who had disappeared or fled, like Campendonck and Klee (*GD*, 12.11.36), and those who were in disgrace (Marc, Werfel, Nolde, Feininger,

Kirschner, Pechstein, Heckel, Grosz, Dix, Kandinsky, Schmidt-Rottluff, Baumeister, Bargheer, Barlach, *GD*, 10.11.36, 3.2.37). Beckett knew, too, that writers were suffering a similar fate. He learnt in October that the works of Heinrich Mann were no longer obtainable; then, in January, that Heinrich's brother Thomas's had also been banned (*GD*, 28.10.36, 11.1.37). He heard that other authors were also on the blacklist: Sauerlandt, Werner Mahrholz, Stefan and Anton Zweig (*GD*, 28.10.36, 2.11.36). He was advised not to read expelled authors (*GD*, 22.10.36) or certain histories of art and literature.

He knew that, whilst paintings were disappearing from gallery walls and being stuffed in cellars (*GD*, 30.10.36), it was sometimes possible to make a clandestine arrangement to see them. This, when he could, he did. He got the British Consulate in Hamburg to produce a letter supporting him in his efforts to see 'forbidden' art in the Kunsthalle and the Museum für Kunst und Gewerbe. (The letter arrived too late to be of use.)[31] He also visited private collections. He sought out painters and art historians, talked and listened to them. Quite a lot of the diary entries consist to some extent of lists: painters' full names (underlined), often with their dates, their nationalities or places of origin, the schools to which they belonged. Sometimes the lists include titles of pictures. Beckett briefly describes certain pictures but not others. On occasions, he repeats details from one entry to another. He himself seems at one point depressed and exasperated by how far his diaries consist of such lists, and takes it to be a sign of obsessional neurosis (*GD*, 2.2.37). They served no purpose, he thought. Yet he also drew elaborate plans of floors in museums (the Kaiser Friedrich Museum and the Altes Museum in Berlin, the Alte Pinakothek in Munich, *GD*, 2.1.37, 27.12.36, 8.3.37), some-times numbering the rooms. He sketched the screen of the western choir in the cathedral at Naumburg and the Goldene Pforte at the Freiberg cathedral, carefully noting the position of the figures (*GD*,

19.2.37). He drew a ground-plan of the Wallfahrtskirche at Staffe-stein (*GD*, 22.2.37). Once again, at such moments, he seems less concerned with art criticism than simply recording what is there, as though fearful it might soon be proscribed, or simply cease to be.

Beckett was obviously drawn into sympathy with German Jews, a sympathy he expressed in different ways, some more conscious or direct than others. He remarks on the desolation of the Jüdischer Friedhof in Hamburg (*GD*, 15.10.37). He notes his particular liking for a casual Jewish acquaintance, Professor Benno Diederich, and for another he remarks is married to a Jew, a stage decorator called Porep (*GD*, 25.10.36, 23.1.37). He made special efforts to meet and talk to Jews like Schapire and Will Grohmann, sacked director of the Zwinger Gallery in Dresden (a man sufficiently intellectual and brave to think, and tell Beckett, that it was more interesting

'A haunting beauty': Jacob von Ruisdael's 17th-century *The Jewish Cemetery*.

to stay in Germany than to leave it, *GD*, 2.2.37). He took a particular interest in Jewish artists and art critics, like Wohlwill (*GD*, 24.11.36). He even sold what he had started to call his *Hitlermantel*, his leather coat (*GD*, 4.12.36, 13.2.37), and had a new suit made from materials supplied by Jewish dealers (*GD*, 23.2.37). At times, his disquiet emerges obliquely, as when he notes of Jacob van Ruisdael's hauntingly beautiful painting *The Jewish Cemetery* that it may have been burnt by now (*GD*, 15.10.36). Whilst neither Jewish nor immediately concerned with Jews, Helene Fera, Chair of the University's International Relations Office, the Akademische Auslandstelle, refused to be bullied by the Nazis and served as a crucial nexus for international student contacts in Hamburg. The most beguiling photograph in Roswitha Quadflieg's account of Beckett's weeks in Hamburg shows Fera, in 1936, pointedly surrounded by students of different races, notably Asians. Beckett thought of her as 'the best of her generation, that I have met and will meet in this or almost any other land'.[32]

Beyond all this, however, an intention hidden from Beckett also draws him into a different and more complex expression of sympathy. From the start of his trip, he conceives of Germany as bursting with poisons, thick with waste matter. When he heard Hitler and Goebbels' speeches at the opening of the *Winterhilfswerk*, just four days after his arrival, he wrote that they would have to fight, 'or burst' (*GD*, 6.10.36).[33] Wherever he turns, he runs into shit. The German press is full of it (*GD*, 3.1.37). Strangely, compulsively, his fastidiously sensitive body responds in kind. When he dismisses the notion of the German *Schicksal*, he adds that 'the expressions "historical necessity" and "Germanic destiny" start the vomit moving upwards'.[34] Attacks on modernist art in the press make him want to puke (*GD*, 15.1.37).

The theme of purging oneself of noxious waste is only partly metaphorical. It is also literal, physical. Beckett's body starts to mimic the disorder he perceives around him. Thus 'bursting' is

Eating well was an integral part of Nazi self-congratulation, as in this drawing in a February 1937 issue of the ss weekly paper *Das Schwarze Korps*. At the same time, Beckett was finding himself increasingly revolted by German food.

Im Zeichen des Eintopfes

a word that recurs throughout the diaries. He repeatedly describes himself as bursting with wind or bursting for a piss or a shit. He suffers from diarrhoea, he fouls himself, he vomits. To anyone familiar with foreign travel on a limited budget, this may not seem very remarkable. What is remarkable is the repetitiveness of the details, their variety and the pains that Beckett takes to note them. That he pays them such sedulous attention suggests that he sees them as integral to his German experience as a whole. He has a pus-filled finger and thumb which he has to lance himself. He discovers lumps and boils under his scrotum and in his anus which seem eerily like fungoid growths. They also burst. His gorge rises. He experiences nausea. In Hitler's Munich, not long before his departure, he abruptly declares that German food is awful, and, having eaten in Germany for several months, repeatedly wonders where one could possibly find food that one might stomach (*GD*, 9.3.37), eventually abbreviating the question, What can one eat? to the acronym w.c.o.e. (10.3.37).

However obscurely, Beckett knew very well that Germany was caught up in convulsions, and about to convulse the world, with unpredictable but fearful consequences. He endured convulsions of his own. In London, he had gone to Bion partly because of physical symptoms which analysis seemed to alleviate, if not partially cure. However, Germany subjected him to physical upheaval all over again. His body became an inert cadaver that he had to drag out on to the streets in the morning. He frequently describes himself as crawling. He suffered repeated outbreaks of herpes on his lip. A raw wound on his back made him fear he might have VD (*GD*, 7.2.37). He was troubled by pains in his penis (*GD*, 5.3.37). The *German Diaries* make it harder to see Beckett's physical condition in common-sense terms, as psychosomatic. His symptoms begin to seem more like manifestations of an almost terrifying susceptibility to the world around him. But he holds this exposure at one remove; hence his occasional pro-fessions of deadened feeling. All the same, he suffers. He suffers hopelessly, involuntarily and abjectly, because any other response would spell his own derogation. He suffers stoically, but with an agonized and almost spiritual intensity. His pain and wretched-ness are at times appalling, and very moving.

Just five days before he left Germany (*GD*, 28.3.37), he bought a great novel, Grimmelshausen's *Simplicissimus*, remarkable for its magnificent, sombre if richly comic treatment of a Germany shat-tered (by the Thirty Years War). In 'The Calmative' (1946), Beckett would later also read 'the contemporary landscape' with reference to that particular European cataclysm.[35] In early 1937, he wanders cheerlessly through a morally devastated landscape, one that would in due course of time be literally laid waste. He foresaw the likelihood of this, writing to MacGreevy of the possible destruction of Europe as early as October, 1936.[36] At one particular moment in the diaries, so powerful as to seem almost vatic, Karl Schmidt-Rottluff's portrait of Rosa Schapire leads him to a conception of art as prayer; prayer, that is, which 'sets up prayer', releasing prayer in another. As he himself succinctly explains: '*Priest*: Lord have mercy upon us. *People*: Christ have mercy upon us'.[37]

The Beckett astray in Nazi Germany, however, assumed the role less of priest than scapegoat, the 'escape-goat', the goat that, on the Day of Atonement, leaves the city, burdened with the sins of the people.[38] To assimilate Beckett, here, however, in this precise context, to the Jewish scapegoat is to run the risk of a trivialization that he would himself have scrupulously deplored. In any case, it is not the Jewish scapegoat that Beckett in Germany most calls to mind, but the ancient Greek *pharmakos*.[39] The *pharmakos* was often associated with poetry (Aesop, Hipponax, Tyrtaeus). He was 'that

'Christ have mercy upon us': Karl Schmidt-Rottluff's *Rosa Schapire*, 1919.

which is thrown away in cleansing'. He was polluted, and bore 'the plague of shame' in a time of communal disaster.[40] He might do so voluntarily (whatever will means, in this context). According to the most famous theorist of the scapegoat, René Girard, the *pharmakos* particularly appeared in times of violent conflict.[41] He might be a foreigner (like the Cretan Androgeus in Athens) and have suffered a peripety from best to worst. The *pharmakoi* were *rejecta*: ugly, misshapen, foul. But they might also be the best of men, sacred figures, supreme (like Aesop) at intellectual pursuits. They were bearers of poison, but also the remedy for it.

It is the Irish equivalent of the *pharmakos*, however, that supplies the most arresting analogy to Beckett's plight in Germany.[42] Like other *pharmakoi*, though he might draw close to it and seek to exploit it, the Irish blame poet was implacably contemptuous of power. He was irreducibly at odds with it, in all its dispersed and winding ways, not least, when it was the power of a community united. Hence, sooner or later, he necessarily became an exile or outlaw. But he was also a *histrion*. His body mimed out what he saw. The shame, blemish and disgrace he perceived returned upon him. He might be leprous or otherwise diseased. He was often physically loathsome. At all events, the one invariable feature of the stories of the *pharmakoi* is their eventual departure from the city or fatherland. The *German Diaries* close as soon as Beckett leaves Germany. But according to *Leviticus* (16.22) the goat 'shall bear upon him all their iniquities unto a land not inhabited', that is, into the wilderness. For many years to come, artistically at least, the wilderness was to be Beckett's home.

5

Élimination des déchets: The War, Resistance, Vichy France, 1939–44

From Germany, on 1 April 1937, Beckett returned to Ireland, home and scrapping with his mother. He was chronically adrift, or, as he put it himself, 'deterioriating now very rapidly'.[1] There is a story of him crawling drunkenly from under a table at a party, having vainly pestered his hostess for sexual favours.[2] This seems indicative of his state of mind. Not surprisingly, he was reading about the eminently stoic sufferer Samuel Johnson, and that gloomiest of philosophers, Schopenhauer, deciding that 'he was one of the ones that mattered most to me'.[3] There was really nothing left for him in Ireland. 'Even mother suggests my leaving this country', he wrote, '*une fois pour toutes*'.[4]

Crucially, the final break came, and was sealed, as a result of two confrontations with Irish authorities and institutions. Firstly, Beckett had another car accident. No one was hurt, but the Gardai prosecuted him for dangerous driving. Beckett disputed the charge, declaring in the process that there was no animal he loathed 'more profoundly than a civic guard, a symbol of [post–1922] Ireland with his official, loutish Gaelic complacency'.[5] If 'there is a definite note of Foxrock unionism' about this prejudice,[6] there was equally a note of recrudescent Anglo-Irish *lèse-majesté* about the second confrontation. Beckett's uncle Harry Sinclair had claimed that, in his recently published memoir, *As I Was Going Down Sackville Street*, Oliver St John Gogarty had characterized his grandfather as a usurer. Sinclair filed a libel suit against Gogarty, and Beckett agreed to appear as a witness for the prosecution. In October, he left Ireland for Paris. He came back in November, when the case was brought.

Beckett had his reasons for siding as he did, though he was no doubt more conscious of some of them than others. Joyce had thought of Gogarty as one of his principal Irish betrayers. Yet it is hard not to feel that there was more than loyalty to Joyce or his uncle at stake in Beckett's role in Gogarty's downfall (for Sinclair eventually won, and Gogarty had to leave Ireland as a result). Gogarty came from an affluent Catholic middle-class background. He was a sleek figure with a country house and a Rolls-Royce (both of which he lost in the case). He had supported the Free State, served as a Senator and successfully established himself on the Dublin literary scene. His star had therefore been in the ascendant whilst Beckett's had appeared to sink. More generally, the rise of Gogarty's class had been proportional to the decline of Beckett's. From Beckett's point of view, this clearly lent a certain edge to the situation. But he also had to endure the contumely of defending counsel John Mary Fitzgerald, his crass sneers at what he saw as the Frenchified, atheistic decadence of a '"bawd and blasphemer" from Paris',[7] his satirical reading aloud from *More Pricks than Kicks*, and his gloating reference to its falling foul of the Irish censor.

If Beckett had been in any doubt as to where his roots now lay, Fitzgerald must have smothered it for good. From the end of 1937 to the outbreak of the war, he began to shift his ground. He went back to Paris and its literary circles, to Joyce and the avant-garde. At the same time, he was now finding it difficult to write about Joyce, as the *Nouvelle revue française* had asked him to. Then, in early January, whilst out with friends in the fourteenth *arrondissement*, he was stabbed by a pimp who had been pestering them. He was taken to hospital, where the Joyces and other friends pampered him. One of his visitors was Suzanne Deschevaux-Dumesnil. Suzanne was an interesting woman, a *gauchiste* with Communist friends and a social conscience. Beckett had known her slightly since his time at the École Normale. Once he emerged from hospital, they grew close. Since the American heiress Peggy Guggenheim was also competing for his attention, it might seem as though he was caught on the horns of a dilemma. But whatever the other factors involved, Beckett was never likely to choose wealth and privilege. Suzanne prevailed, and the relationship flourished. She was to be the most important woman in Beckett's later life.

Beckett was hardly about to abandon Joyce. The reverse: not only did he more and more recognize the deep streak of humility and self-abnegation in the great writer; he also increasingly saw him as an ordinarily lovable man. All the same, between 1937 and 1940, Joyce and Suzanne represented the twin poles in Beckett's life, with Beckett himself gravitating from one to the other. It was ever more clear that even Joyce's identification with Ireland at one remove was not going to work for the younger Anglo-Irishman. Beckett began to write poetry in French, asserting that any future poems would probably be in French, too. With hindsight, this looks almost like a declaration of allegiance. He was 'already evolving in 1938–9 specifically into a *French* writer'.[8] He turned to writing in French as the language of his actual historical situation – for Beckett, immediate historical experience repeatedly manifested itself in and as language. He committed himself to Suzanne at the same point in time. Then, on 18 April 1939, just two weeks after de Valera had visited Mussolini in Rome and ten days after the Dáil Éireann had discussed the Irish policy of neutrality in European affairs, Beckett wrote that 'If there is a war, and I fear there must be soon, I shall place myself at the disposition of this country';[9] by which, of course, he meant France. When war was declared, he was in Ireland, but set out immediately for Paris.

The Second World War began in September 1939. In May 1940, Hitler invaded France and the Low Countries. The German

Blitzkrieg was devastatingly effective, and France surrendered on 22 June. For the French, the war was brief and disastrous, with 90,000 dead and nearly two million soldiers taken prisoner. But if the defeat was unexpected and humiliating, the German occupation was still more so. The country's institutions fell apart. The *Wehrmacht* took over the north of France, and a new French government constituted itself in Vichy, in the unoccupied south, but with legal authority in both the northern and the 'free zone'. Led by Marshal Philippe Pétain, it referred to itself as the French State, not the Republic, and to its reactionary programme as the National Revolution. Meanwhile, the French Resistance began its operations against both the Nazis and Vichy. In London, General Charles de Gaulle disputed the legitimacy of Vichy France and Pétain's leadership, and claimed to incarnate the very spirit of France. De Gaulle's Free French Forces carried on the struggle alongside British troops and in the French colonies. They joined in the Allied invasion of France, incorporating the Resistance as the French Forces of the Interior. Upon the dissolution of the Vichy regime, in June 1944, de Gaulle proclaimed the Provisional Government of the French Republic.

Our picture of France between 1940 and 1949, however, is no longer quite what it was. The flowering of Beckett criticism coincided with a revolution in the historical study of modern France of which Beckettians have so far taken little account.[10] The 'Paxtonian revolution'[11] – initiated by the great American scholar Robert O. Paxton, and subsequently fomented by Maurice Rajsfus, Dominique Veillon, Henry Rousso, Roderick Kedward, Pierre Azéma and others – has had profound implications for French culture, chiefly in the past two decades. Among other developments, it led, for example, to the longest trial in French history, that of Maurice Papon, which finally ended in 1998, and at which some of the historians gave evidence; and, most starkly of all, in 1995, to President Jacques Chirac's formal acknowledgement of the support the French State had given to the 'criminal folly' of the Nazis and, in its deportation of Jews, to the Final Solution.[12] The Paxtonian revolution markedly changes the meaning of a set of terms (Vichy, the Resistance, the *maquis*, Gaullism, collaboration and so on) which define the period of French history in which Beckett came to prominence as a French writer. Unless we see him in relation to the work of these historians – as, in 1940–44, wandering through and surviving in a degraded France, then, in the late 1940s, devising his masterpiece, the *Trilogy*, in a France that had torn itself apart – we don't quite get him at all.

The Liberation brought with it a relatively benign interpretation of the Nazi occupation of France that was well established by the 1950s and 'supported by popular and scholarly opinion until the 1970s'.[13] If, after 1945, France was inclined to mourn its recent past, political contradictions swiftly brought that process to a halt. These contradictions proved to be insuperable.[14] Since reason could not resolve them, the French turned to myth. The mythic narrative presented the Vichy years as a historical parenthesis in which the French had been forced to compromise with a monstrous evil. According to this fable, Pétain had manfully shielded his country from a fate far grimmer than mere occupation. However, a small cabal of collaborators, notably prime minister Pierre Laval, had betrayed him and increasingly co-operated with the Nazis. Aside from the cabal and a few sympathizers, the French nation had been united in stubborn hostility and often active resistance to the invader.

The Paxtonian historians have shattered this myth. Vichy saw the French defeat as the result of the decay of the Republic, above all, under the leftist Popular Front in the 1930s. Its mission was therefore to regenerate France, not least by suppressing the 'impure elements' responsible for the alleged decay. It is now clear, for example, that Vichy repeatedly offered the Germans more assistance than they actually requested, notably with regard to the deportation of French Jews and the transportation of French workers. Vichy even sued to be part of Hitler's New Order, but was turned down by the Führer himself. The consequence of Vichy policy, however, was deep division. In fact, France was riven by the occupation, and the rifts snake their way through French society till this day. According to Rousso, occupied France was actually in a state of savage 'civil war', notably but by no means only between Pétain's paramilitary Milice and the Communists and Resistance.[15]

The historians, however, have also repeatedly shown that the old labels, like resistance and collaboration themselves, designate not homogeneous categories, but highly differentiated and ambivalent entities. There were 'Vichyist-resisters', for example. Many individuals changed allegiance very quickly during the progress of the war. Some historians have even questioned, or at least radically complicated, what Jean-Marie Guillon calls the 'legendary' history of the *maquis*,[16] the armed resistance in the hills and forests, of which Beckett had some knowledge and a little experience. True, one or two scholars have recently also begun to wonder whether the concept of a uniformly myth-driven postwar France should not itself be questioned.[17] It is nonetheless the case that the spectre of Vichy has yet to be altogether exorcized. As Conan and Rousso put matters, borrowing a phrase from German historian Emil Nolte, far from being an unfortunate historical aberration now mercifully buried, Vichy is a *Vergangenheit, die nicht vergangen will*, a past that refuses to lie down and die.[18]

Beckett's wartime journey took him through a wide range of experiences of France, from the German occupation of Paris to the Resistance, Vichy France, the *maquis*, the Allied invasion and the Liberation. At the start of the war, he offered to drive an ambulance, but events overtook him. By early June, having neatly outflanked the Maginot line, the *Wehrmacht* was powering its way towards Paris. As the French government fled to Tours, so, too, Beckett and Suzanne fled, arriving in Vichy itself on 12 June. There they joined the Joyces in the Hôtel Beaujolais, which, by a quaint irony, was soon to be commandeered by government ministers, including Beckett's old friend Georges Pelorson, who was to direct Vichy's youth propaganda progamme. Pelorson was in Vichy when Beckett arrived, but his extreme views meant that their relationship had already cooled. From Vichy, Beckett and Suzanne travelled to Toulouse, along with many others in flight from the invader. Beckett possessed no formal proof of his nationality or status, and therefore ran the risk of 'being detained indefinitely as an unregistered alien'.[19] From Toulouse, he and Suzanne headed for Bordeaux, but were dumped at night in a rainswept Cahors, where Suzanne collapsed from exhaustion, and Beckett wept. They moved on to Arcachon. For all the presence of German troops, Beckett might have lived there comparatively untroubled. But it was not where his ties or his loyalties lay. So, in September, he and Suzanne returned to Paris.

Once back in the capital, of course, they had to bear with its despondency, its ration queues, its meagre resources and its German-controlled police. Many of Beckett's old friends had left and not returned. But this was not the case with Alfred Péron. Péron introduced Beckett to the Resistance network known as 'Gloria SMH'. It is characteristic of Beckett that he should have later played his Resistance work down and attached no great importance to it. He no doubt joined the Resistance partly because of his appalled awareness of the Nazis' treatment of the Jews (including, more and more, Parisian Jews). He also did it out of loyalty to friends. At the same time, it is important that he came to Resistance work *via* a *normalien*. French historians repeatedly emphasize how far, for men like Péron, joining the Resistance meant 'a commitment made out of principle', an act of faith, 'a bet from which there was nothing to gain' and which therefore ran counter to common sense.[20] In this sense at least, the famous *résistant* Emmanuel d'Astier de la Vigerie was right to claim that 'one could only be a resister if one was maladjusted'.[21] For the intellectual turned fighter, working for the Resistance also meant an intellectual choice, made according to an intellectual logic. In the case of *normaliens*, this logic evolved from the 'granite point' at which, however absurd one might appear, one knew oneself to be morally beyond all compromise. The supreme example of it was that great *normalien* Cavaillès, who was tortured, shot and buried as 'unknown no. 5' in 1944, and with whom Beckett had more in common than is often suspected.

Not that Beckett's work for 'Gloria' was obviously very heroic. His job was to process information provided for him by agents, putting it in order, condensing and translating it so that it could then be miniaturized and sent on to London. Eventually, like Cavaillès' network, 'Gloria' was betrayed, the man responsible being the great villain of the Beckett biography, the monster and churchman Robert Alesch. Beckett and Suzanne narrowly escaped the Gestapo. Others, including Péron, were not so fortunate. Beckett and Suzanne went into hiding in Paris. Their predicament was nerve-racking. A Jewish companion committed suicide. They sought refuge outside Paris with Nathalie Sarraute, with whom Beckett seems to have had a very Sarrautian relationship, thick with tension and half-suppressed dislike. He and Suzanne subsequently escaped to the 'free zone'. They reached Vichy, where Beckett's foreign passport and their lack of valid travel documents left them vulnerable.

Eventually, they arrived in Roussillon in the Vaucluse, not far from Avignon. Roussillon was not occupied by Germans, though there were Germans aplenty nearby, and a former *résistant* was not exactly safe. Nor of course were Jews, and, since either Beckett or Suzanne was often taken for Jewish, this, too, left them at risk. They bunkered down obscurely, making local friends, and worrying like the locals about the availability of food and clothing, especially footwear. They worked on farms, grubbed for potatoes, kept up with the news of Vichy and the war as best they could, and avoided German patrols. They were never far away from a world in which betrayals, denunciations and arbitrary violence were the order of the day. Meanwhile, Beckett worked on the novel *Watt*. In May 1944, he rejoined the Free Forces of the Interior, working with the local *maquisards*. Finally, in August, the Americans liberated the village.

Beckett distilled his wartime experience in his best-known work, the play *En attendant Godot* (*Waiting for Godot*), which he wrote in French in late 1948 and early 1949. As Dominique Veillon's research makes clear, under Vichy, waiting was both a common and a significant experience.[22] In wartime France, one waited interminably, whether it was for *cartes d'alimentation* or parachute drops. The word *attente* was very much a part of the universe of those who worked in the Resistance, and waiting was a constant feature of their everyday life.[23] Beckett himself was clearly familiar with it as such. But the word *attendant* also evokes an attitude that was known as *attentisme*. The term was commonplace in Vichy France. Many if not most of the members of Beckett's original Parisian audiences would have been aware of it.

There were many different positions within Vichy culture regarding the German occupation, involving widely different degrees of support, acquiescence and resistance. The word *attentisme* designated one set of them.[24] *Attentisme* was the attitude of those who did not believe that 'the Pétain experiment' would succeed, but argued that there was no possibility of an immediate return to the battlefield. It was necessary to defer any final decision until the situation 'clarified itself'. France should wait for the right moment 'to jump back into war'.[25] In reality, this frequently meant that it should wait until the Americans were obviously coming out on top. Versions of *attentisme* ranged from mild collaborationism to the cynicism of those aware that it would pay not to be associated with Vichy once the Allies landed. The term also designated stoical or foot-dragging attitudes within the Resistance itself:[26] hence, in part, the historians' revisions of the *maquis* legend. *Attentisme* involved a particular kind of ambiguity, and a particular disposition towards it. Paxton suggests that it was probably the philosophy of the majority of Frenchmen and women under Vichy.[27] To intellectuals, radicals and anti-Fascists, it was the least objectionable position outside the Resistance.[28] The Vichy government hated it.

One reason for this was that *attentisme* flouted if it did not actively oppose Vichy ideology. It took revenge on Petainism on behalf of the obstinately unreconstructed and resiliently common-place strata of Vichy society. For Vichy called for the moral renewal of France.[29] This involved bans on corrupting modern art (like jazz), and occasional book-burnings. It also involved a major programme for 'the physical development and the moral revival of [the] race'.[30] Vichy was notable for its youth movements, its promotion of group activities, physical education and outdoor sports. The aim was to improve the moral fibre of the French, particularly the young, and their sense of unity, discipline, hier-archy and community.[31] Above all, however, as we noted earlier, the Vichy regime wanted to rid France of those marked out as a threat to French morale, the 'impure elements' infesting the nation. The principal 'impurities' were Jews, *métèques*, Freemasons, communists, gypsies, homosexuals and, in general, foreigners both real and 'internal', like Beckett himself. Vichy did it best to intern or deport them. Indigents and the stateless were amongst those most likely to find themselves in camps.

The baleful figure of Alexis Carrel looms particularly large in this. Carrel was a Nobel prizewinner and celebrity. He was also the guiding spirit of the Fondation Française pour l'Étude des Problèmes Humaines, created by Vichy decree in November 1941 to study, safeguard, improve and develop the French population via an 'experimental science of man'.[32] Carrel was a eugenicist. He was intent on countering what he took to be the organic decay of the French nation. He urged that this be effected by eugenic means. He argued the need for voluntary or forced sterilization or confinement for those suffering from natal insanity, maniac and depressive psychoses, hereditary epilepsy, blindness and other serious defects.[33] Carrel went so far as to advocate gas chambers as a means of ridding humanity of its 'inferior stock'.[34] He enthusiastically praised the German government for its treatment of criminals and the mentally defective and diseased, and advocated the 'suppression' of such degenerate life-forms as soon as they proved 'dangerous'.[35] He promoted the anthropological study of peasants and immigrants (who were categorizable as either 'desirable' or 'undesirable') to help determine the ethnic features best suited to the French.

That Beckett was conscious of the invidiousness of Vichy policy, and probably also of Carrel, is clear from Lucky's great monologue in *En attendant Godot*. Critics have often read this as absurdist gobbledygook. In fact, a rigorous moral logic underpins it. It is in large measure a *reductio ad absurdum* of Vichy ideology. The monologue takes, as its principal points of reference, empty academic or pseudo-scientific discourses of knowledge and discourses of cultural 'improvement'. These clearly bear traces of Vichy: Lucky talks of 'la culture physique de la pratique des sports' (*EAG*, p. 38); 'augmentation' and élimination' (ibid.) were key terms in the discourses dominant in Carrel's *Fondation*. So, too, Lucky's phrase 'élimination des déchets' suggests elimination of social trash as well as physical waste matter (ibid.). Whilst the nonsense Lucky produces is comic and even satirical, it also insists that Vichyite and eugenicist discourses are at best irrelevant to and at worst a noxious violation of limited, deficient, suffering human being. In effect, the monologue is a defence of indigent forms of humanity or, in Agamben's terms, 'bare life'.[36]

The historians of the Paxtonian revolution finally provide us with a description of Vichy France as profoundly traumatized, both

A contemporary cartoon commenting on poverty under the Vichy regime.

by defeat and by Vichy policy itself. 'All that remains', said painter Jean Bazaine, in 1942, 'is man confronting life'.[37] 'Everything was called into question', writes Veillon.[38] Jean-Pierre Rioux describes the culture of wartime France as one of 'sufferings and privations', 'nomadic wanderings', 'all-too-obvious tragedies and ruined hopes' – but also unexpected freedoms of thought.[39] Marjorie Perloff argues very strikingly that Beckett's *Stories* are about this condition.[40] But to many of his French contemporaries, it was his great play, above all, that seemed to capture it exactly. *En attendant Godot* is rooted in life under Vichy, as Veillon's account makes clear. Cartoons of broken-down bourgeois who look like tramps appear in the newspapers of the period.[41] The concern with cold, footwear, 'nourritures terrestres', small scraps of that rarity, meat, violence perpetrated on outcasts, travel restrictions or the lack of them; the obsession with 'faits anodins', with the experience of being 'engluée dans une banalité journalière': all are in the play, and all were commonplace aspects of Vichy life, as they were of Beckett's and Suzanne's.[42] So, too, were random manifestations of peremptory and brutal power, as embodied in the play in the

La carte de vêtements.
— Est-ce que je grogne, moi ? Pas du tout ! J'use mes vieux complets...

'Broken-down bourgeois who look like tramps' in another Vichy cartoon.

relationship between Pozzo and Lucky. Beckett lodges *En attendant Godot* in a specific experience of historical deprivation.

More importantly, the play refuses to look beyond that experience. It rather insists on its significance, as opposed to the discourses of a bankrupt positivity. It offers us no superior perspective on and does not attempt to redeem the experience of deprivation. Beckett's bleak, rich, abundant laughter identifies with collapsed and impotent creatures, with beings at the limits of their feeble capacities, with the myriad forms of depletion. The play takes an extravagant delight in *Unfähigkeit*, the fact of not being able, in the radical imperfection of 'impure elements'. It resists any temptation to make practical use of uselessness. That is why political moralists like Brecht so distrusted it. In relishing a degree zero of point and purpose, in turning ordinary futility into a source of ample pleasure, *En attendant Godot* performs one of the most hallowed functions reserved for art. The same identification also makes the play *attentiste*, if comically and ironically. For all his own work with the Resistance, in *En attendant Godot* Beckett deliberately refuses to look beyond *attentisme* (which seems cognate with the fact that he set his work as a *résistant* at naught). This attitude was clearly connected to his experience in Roussillon. In all these respects, *Godot* is a fierce rejoinder to the inflated, humourless, inanely vicious discourses of Vichy ideology.

But it also stands haplessly against another drive. In the end, the suspect positivities at stake in the play are not merely Vichy's. Beckett wrote the play in a climate of pompous Gaullist triumphalism, vigorous protestations of a morality of *engagement* (a term which Sartre had first put into circulation in 1945) and the cultural cleansing involved in the self-righteous and vindictive persecution of those thought to have worked with the enemy. France was determined to rid itself of shame, thereby swiftly achieving historical amnesia. Meanwhile, Carrel's Fondation discreetly converted itself into the handsomely funded Institut National d'Études Démographiques, and continued and developed certain aspects of his work, still existing to this day. To understand this context, and grasp Beckett's writings of the late 1940s as a response to it, we need to retrace our steps.

6

Indignités: Liberation,
the Purge, de Gaulle, 1944–9

Beckett and Suzanne returned to Paris in November 1944,[1] and
went back to their former apartment, which now bore traces
of being searched by the Gestapo. Beckett described the Paris
of the time as 'grim'.[2] He sent his brother an eminently Beckettian
telegram informing him that it was 'IMPOSSIBLE TO MOVE AT
PRESENT'.[3] It was logical that he should have thought so. If his
personal circumstances were not encouraging, nor were political
conditions in Paris. But Beckett wanted to get back to Ireland, so
he did move, after all, on 8 April. England greeted him as warmly
as it had in the past. Immigration officials confiscated his passport,
and the War Office asked him to explain his wartime absence from
Britain. In London, he wandered through bomb-shattered land-
scapes. When he reached Ireland, however, like a man who feels
set apart by his recent history, he steered clear of his former
acquaintance. His sense of his own distance from them only
increased when he heard the news of the death of his *normalien*
friend and fellow *résistant* Péron in the concentration camp at
Mauthausen. Soon he was ready to leave the British Isles again.

Fascinatingly, however, in spite of his decisive turn to France,
the circumstances of his departure once again expressed some
of the ambivalences of an Anglo-Irishman after Independence.
In Dublin, he was very conscious of what seemed like Irish
abundance, as contrasted with French deprivation. 'My friends',
he remarked, pointedly meaning Frenchmen and women, 'eat

sawdust and turnips while all of Ireland safely gorges'.[4] It was
as though he were repeating the declaration of allegiance he had
made in 1939. He was clearly unimpressed by Ireland's neutral
position during the war.[5] Yet, at the same time, his next move
brought him into line with de Valera himself. In a speech he
broadcasted on VE day, Winston Churchill referred contemptu-
ously to Irish neutrality. De Valera was not about to let this stand.
On 16 May 1945 he responded, in what many Irishmen and women
took to be his finest moment on the radio. Ireland's task came now.
'As a community which has been mercifully spared from all the
major sufferings', said de Valera,

> as well as from the blinding hates and rancours engendered
> by the present war, we shall endeavour to render thanks to
> God by playing a Christian part in helping, so far as a small
> nation can, to bind up the wounds of suffering humanity.[6]

Beckett would hardly have seen himself as an emissary of the
Taoiseach. Still less would he have been inclined to render thanks
to God. Nonetheless, in early August, he joined 'the Irish bringing
gifts' (CSP, p. 276), enrolling with the Irish Red Cross, and setting
off for Saint-Lô.

The French called Saint-Lô 'the capital of ruins'. The new arrival
confronted a mind-numbing panorama of wreckage. 'No lodging
of course of any kind', wrote Beckett, in the clipped, sepulchral
tone that so many of his characters would soon be speaking in.[7]
Yet human creatures were surviving amidst the debris, scuttling
out from cellars and scavenging amidst the ubiquitous mud. If
this called certain scenes from Irish history to mind, it would not
have been surprising. Beckett no doubt witnessed other horrors,
or at least, their consequences. In 'The Capital of Ruins', written
for Radio Éireann in June 1946, he talked about the frequent acci-
dents resulting from falling masonry and children playing with

detonators. He told MacGreevy that one of the Red Cross priorities was a VD clinic. By 1945, the war had made sexually transmitted diseases a crucial issue, not least because of the incidence of prostitution and rape. At all events, Saint-Lô was a place to learn, or to know yet again, that '"provisional" is not the term it was, in this universe become provisional' (*CSP*, p. 278).

'All is dark', says Moran in *Molloy*, 'but with that simple darkness that follows like a balm upon the great dismemberings' (*TR*, p. 111). If any balm was to hand in France in 1945, events soon dissipated it. Beckett stayed in Saint-Lô until December 1945. Then he returned to Paris. Paris was home. There was no question of feeling distant from it. Indeed, Beckett had kept on making trips to Paris from Normandy. Since its liberation, however, by Allied Operation Overlord, in August 1944, Paris had become a special kind of beast. So, for that matter, had France. The Liberation was quickly followed by the Purge.[8] The Purge is most notorious for the shaving

The *épuration sauvage*: Frenchmen take their revenge on perceived collaborators with the German occupiers.

of the heads of Frenchwomen supposed to have consorted with the enemy. In actual fact, it was a far more protracted and complex phenomenon than a single image can suggest. There were at least three stages to it. In the first and most obviously shocking, the *épuration sauvage*, which included the shavings, outraged Frenchmen and women, some of whom had not been much less complicit with the Germans than their victims, nonetheless took revenge – on occasions, murderously – on those they deemed to have been collaborators. Some of the direst features of Vichy France – special courts, internments, denunciations, arbitrary arrests, atrocities as committed by Pétain's paramilitary Milice, even torture – were duly maintained in the hands of its enemies. Improvised courts martial took place. Collaborators were held on the very sites where Vichy had detained French Jews. The widespread practice of 'popular justice' might mean execution without trial. Its victims died in the street, in their houses or at the hands of lynch mobs. Sartre thought that France was in danger of collapsing into 'mediaeval sadism'.[9]

The *épuration légale* that followed the initial barbarisms, however, was scarcely a paradigm of justice restored. De Gaulle was now the President of the Provisional Government of the French Republic. The Gaullists had established a purge committee as early as 1943, to provide a legal system for the trial of collaborators. In 1944, before France had a new constitution or the French had elected a new parliament, they instituted new courts of justice. The new juridical formulations were extremely severe. 'Rarely have such authoritarian provisions been instituted by a regime founded under the sign of liberty', wrote the distinguished historian Robert Aron.[10] Those responsible for the provisions in question were particularly concerned to simplify the arrangements and procedures of previous French court systems, with one judge as opposed to the traditional three, and six jurors as opposed to twelve. At the same time, Gaullists, Communists and socialists all used the courts for political

The trial of Vichy Prime Minister Pierre Laval, October 1945.

ends. Travesties of justice were bound to result, the most egregious instance being the Laval trial. Laval's conduct was hardly defensible. At the same time, his trial was a charade. Witnesses went unheard in the pre-trial interrogation. Crates of evidence were left unopened. Some of the statements read out did not even concern Laval. Jurors bawled at him: 'Bastard!' 'You'll get a dozen bullets!' 'You'll yell less loudly in a fortnight!'.[11] So unedifying was the spectacle that it prompted at least one Jewish journalist to take Laval's side.[12]

The Gaullists also invented a new concept, *indignité nationale*. They wanted it to cover acts of collaboration not previously speci-fied as crimes. It did not imply collusion with the enemy, or even the breaking of a law. In certain circumstances, the guilty party needed only to have made 'scandalous' remarks.[13] The concept of *indignité nationale* declared that what mattered was not what one had done under Vichy, but what one was supposed to have been. The punishment was *dégradation nationale*: shame, loss of status, the proclamation of one's 'unworthiness'. Unfortunately, at the time, French political and judicial *praxis* and the attitudes of many Frenchmen and women markedly lacked the sense of principle that might have ensured the moral credibility of such concepts. Local people and press frequently influenced courtroom proceedings. Juries were blatantly packed. Judges passed sentences that were harsh and undiscriminating to the point of being dismayingly unjust. Even the battle-hardened General Eisenhower was genuinely shocked. It was hard to tell where 'national degradation' began and ended. Apart from appalled crusaders like Jean Paulhan, few seemed truly to rise above it. France itself was writhing in agony at its own recent indignity.

Certainly, in a third phase, the Purge became less draconian. By 1949, the Court of Justice was less in evidence, and judges were more likely to suspend sentences or make them more lenient. De Gaulle and others distributed pardons and amnesties. Increasingly, people agreed that the Gaullists had not constituted the courts with due care and forethought. Thus Pétain himself, whose trial came later, did not meet with the same fate as Laval. Purge victims started telling their stories. The authorities discreetly rehabilitated some of them. In 1950, the Union pour la Restauration et la Défense du Service Public formally condemned the postwar French government, declaring that it had created a repressive apparatus without precedent in history which had attacked free speech, punished political error, stifled freedom of thought and assembly, accepted retroactive legislation and rejected the principle of criminal intent. This was both a soberingly clear-eyed assessment of recent mal-practice, and a token in itself that matters were on the mend. When the Amnesty Bills of 1951 and 1953 came into effect, the process of relaxation was in some respects complete.

But reprieves can be unjust, too. Perhaps the most obvious example of this in post-war France was Papon. During the war, Papon had regularly collaborated with the ss in its persecution of the Jews in the Gironde. De Gaulle apparently knew this. Nonetheless, though Papon was censured after the war, he bounced back, eventually rising as high as Minister of the Budget under Giscard d'Estaing. His recovery was quite typical of the later stages of the Purge. Falsifications of recent history became common. Petainists quietly re-installed themselves in French society. Neo-Vichyites increasingly thrived. Former Vichy officials claimed they had been trying to protect France and French civilians from the Occupation and Nazi policies. They even asserted that, by not promptly handing French Jews over to the Nazis, Vichy had actually done what it could to protect them.

In any case, collaborators were not the only ones who were busily rewriting contemporary history. It was de Gaulle above all who was responsible for the post-war myth of heroic France. In a famous speech of 25 August 1944[14] he played down Allied involvement in the Liberation. He spoke rather of a Paris freed by its own people 'with help from the armies of France, with the help and support of the whole of France, of France which is fighting, of the only France, the real France, eternal France'. He minimized the evils of Vichy, even though the regime itself had condemned him to death for treason. De Gaulle admitted that 'a few unhappy traitors' had given themselves over to the enemy. He could hardly do otherwise. But the Resistance had been heroic, and the majority of the French had conducted themselves as 'bons français'. They had liberated themselves by their own sterling efforts. According to historian Robert Gildea, the 'mythic power' of this gospel was extraordinary.[15] It persisted far beyond de Gaulle's resignation (in 1946). Nearly four decades later, Marguerite Duras could still quote in anger de Gaulle's eminently un-Beckettian message: '"The time for tears is over, the time of glory has returned"'.[16]

For Duras, these words were 'criminal'. 'We will never forgive him', she wrote. De Gaulle declared that 'in the moral realm, seeds of dissension exist and must be eliminated at all costs'.[17] His primary concern was the unity of France, even at the expense of historical truth. It was the cause of unity that the Gaullist mythology served. But de Gaulle's purposes were self-defeating. Initially, at least, before it triumphed as the official story, the mythical narrative was bound to produce yet more of the very dissension it was supposed to quash. Questions of justice, guilt and punishment were widely raised and debated in both the national and the provincial press. It is inconceivable that Beckett, a reader of newspapers, was not aware of this. Other versions of recent history soon started competing with the Gaullist narrative, sometimes splitting communities as they did so. But above all, it was the literary world that called the Gaullist project into question. Writers were unlikely to smother dissent. They were much more likely to express and breed it. De Gaulle however, had seen this coming. He was well aware of how crucial the interventions of writers could be. He roundly declared that two kinds of collaborator deserved neither pity nor commutation of the death-sentence: army officers and talented writers.[18]

Not surprisingly, thus, whilst collaborationist lawyers, businessmen and newspaper magnates frequently passed unnoticed or got off scot-free, Gaullist France repeatedly put writers on trial. The blacklist included the names of Montherlant, Céline and Drieu la Rochelle. It also included Jean Giono, though he had helped both Jews and Resistance fighters. That the inspirational publisher Bernard Grasset had brought Proust, Malraux and Mauriac to the attention of the world did not save him from the charge of collaboration on the basis of an anonymous denunciation. The relevant court found Grasset guilty in 1944: he returned to directing his publishing house only in 1950. At the same time, collaborationism also provoked controversy among writers, including Sartre, de

Beauvoir, Camus, Cocteau, Valéry and François Mauriac. Here, again, the 'seeds of dissension' flourished and spread. Novels like Jean-Louis Curtis's *Les forêts de la nuit* (1947) and Jean Dutourd's *Au bon beurre* (1952) examined the question of personal morality under Vichy, whilst others like Marcel Aymé's *Uranus* (1948) turned a critical or satirical eye on French Communists and Resistance heroes. If Beckett had been indifferent to French literary politics between 1944 and 1949 – and therefore to the country at whose 'disposition' he had emphatically placed himself in April 1939, to which, on 4 September of the same year, he so decisively returned, and for whose cause he then chose to work – he would have been very unusual among Francophone novelists.

Beckett knew of much of the worst of what took place in France in the immediately post-war years. He returned to Paris at a time when the atmosphere was one of terror.[19] Under the heading ARRESTS AND PURGINGS, *Figaro* was publishing daily lists and accounts of summary justice and executions. Readers could get similar information in *Combat* and elsewhere. Beckett clearly knew that, ironically enough, others were claiming that the horrors were taking place so that the Nation could 'proceed calmly to heal [its] wounds and rebuild'.[20] In 'La peinture des van Velde ou le Monde et le Pantalon', for example, written soon after the end of the war, he scathingly declared that, though seemingly lacking the humanity mandatory after a cataclysm, the van Veldes' painting in fact contains more of it than 'toutes leurs processions vers un bonheur de mouton sacré'. He clearly did so with the French context and specifically the excesses of the Purge in mind, not least because he added a reference to the painting being stoned ('Je suppose qu'elle sera lapidée', *DI*, pp. 131–2). He was also conscious of the new cult of heroism. As one of those deemed to have contributed most to liberation through participation in the Resistance, he had himself received the Croix de Guerre, in 1945. The citation, signed by de Gaulle, described him as '[a] man of great courage' who 'carried out his work with extreme bravery'.[21] It was not the way he would have seen himself. In any case, the very France that now abounded in heroes and was busily feting returned political deportees was also slighting or ignoring its labour deportees, returning prisoners of war and Jews.

Beckett had already come across one version of the new French chauvinism in Saint-Lô, where the local French wanted Irish supplies but not the Irish.[22] In 'The Capital of Ruins', he stoutly resisted Gaullist Francocentrism, insisting on a kind of part-mutuality. It was 'the combined energies of the home and visiting tempera-ments' that really mattered, 'the establishing of a relation' between the Irish and 'the rare and famous ways of spirit that are the French ways'. For the 'proposition' underlying the pains the Irish took was that 'their way of being we, was not our way and that our way of being they, was not their way' (*CSP*, p. 277). Liberation, however, did not put a speedy end to the privations and constraints from which the French had suffered, and which Beckett and Suzanne shared. The Paris to which Beckett returned from Saint-Lô was a sombre city of darkened buildings and chronic shortages. What he called his poverty had never distressed him before, and would not unduly do so now. But the moral crisis that France itself was undergoing was a different matter. 'The news of France is very depressing, depresses me anyhow', he wrote to MacGreevy, in 1948, just before beginning the *Trilogy*. 'All the wrong things, all the wrong way. It is hard sometimes to feel the France that one clung to, that I still cling to. I don't mean material conditions', he added, with emphasis.[23] If the France Beckett loved seemed in danger of vanishing, this was partly because Vichy cast such a long shadow. Many of the restrictions for which the Vichy government had been responsible simply remained in place after liberation. But it was not merely in the political sphere that 'all the wrong things' were taking place. The rot had entered the most intimate, inward and private spheres of French life. Suspicion was pervasive, and would remain so for some time to come, as the novels of Nathalie Sarraute so powerfully demonstrate. There was widespread corruption, and callous indifference to the recent sufferings of others.

These, then, were the features of Beckett's world as, between early 1946 and January 1950, he immured himself and wrote *Mercier and Camier*, his four *Stories* ('First Love', 'The Expelled', 'The Calmative' and 'The End') and, above all, from May 1947, his great masterpiece, the *Trilogy*. He called this the period of his 'siege in the room'.[24] He would resort to metaphors of the battlefield later, too, as, for example, when he owned a house near the Marne, he described himself as 'struggling' with work in progress in his 'hole in the Marne mud,' or 'crawling up' on it from 'a ditch somewhere near the last stretch'.[25] In the *German Diaries*, he calls his inner world his 'no man's land' and refers to 'phrases rattling like mashinegun [sic] fire in my skull'.[26] Such images are obviously significant, above all, for the *Trilogy*. The *Trilogy* is everywhere haunted by a vocabulary and images that call modern warfare and its consequences to mind: combustion, detonation, upheaval, crawling, scavenging, ambulances, boots, crutches, rations, ramparts, observation posts, guardrooms, hospitalization, annihilation, loss of limbs, amputation, lightlessness, sheltering in holes, violent encounters in forests, battle-cries, cries in the night, murder, immolation, blackouts, amnesias, extermination, regiments, returnees, war pensions, mutilation, enlistment, puttees, disfiguration, dust-clouds, festered wounds, tyrants, craters, mass burial, cenotaphs, greatcoats, memoirs, mud, decomposing flesh, bodies becoming shapeless heaps or living torches, uprooting, dislocation, and above all, ruins, 'leaning things, forever lapsing and crumbling away' (*TR*, p. 40). The protagonists of the *Trilogy* all make halting progress over featureless or shattered terrain.

This amounts to a (by no means exhaustive) draft inventory of one aspect of Beckett's fantasmagoric stock-in-trade in the late

1940s. Indeed, juggle the pieces, and the *Trilogy* supplies one with a clutch of phrases for a hauntingly vivid and wastefully well-told war story. Malone's 'black unforgettable cohorts' that sweep away the blue (*TR*, p. 198); the Unnamable's 'lights gleaming low afar, then rearing up in a blaze and sweeping down on me' (*TR*, p. 352); its 'small rotunda, windowless, but well furnished with loopholes' (*TR*, p. 320): all could be adjusted to such a purpose. The condition of war victims is repeatedly perceptible in the background of the *Trilogy*: the 'burnt alive', rushing about 'in every direction' (*TR*, p. 370); Malone's 'incandescent migraine' ('My head. On fire, full of boiling oil', *TR*, p. 275); the Unnamable's 'nerves torn from the heart of insentience, with the appertaining terror and the cerebellum on fire' (*TR*, p. 352). Malone's reference to the 'noises of the world' having become 'one vast continuous buzzing' (*TR*, p. 207) calls sufferers from shell-shock to mind. If Molloy, Moran, Malone and the Unnamable's world is one beleaguered by 'the inummerable spirits of darkness' (*TR*, p. 12), in which 'everything is going badly, so abominably badly' (*TR*, p. 375), as such, it is clearly conditioned by recent historical and Beckett's own personal experience, if not directly identifiable with them.

So, too, the shadowy world of the Resistance and the Gestapo also leaves its traces in the *Trilogy*. Ciphers, reports, safe places, objectives, missions, garrotting, the rack, interrogators, secrets, agents, false names, beatings, surveillance, betrayal, provisions, prison cells, night patrols, mutual wariness, terrified neighbours, 'deeds of vengeance' (*TR*, p. 131), concealment of relatives, torture by rats, 'peeping and prying' (*TR*, p. 94), furtive whisperings, surreptitious poisonings, instructions from a chief, 'gaffs, hooks, barbs' and 'grapnels' (*TR*, p. 362), gloves worn 'with all the hard hitting' (*TR*, p. 350), confession, especially of names, or 'piping up' (*TR*, p. 378), auditors who 'listen for the moan that never comes' (*TR*, p. 371), writing to order and for collection (as Beckett did for Gloria): all make their appearance, in some form or another.

Moran declares himself to be 'the faithful servant . . . of a cause that is not mine' (*TR*, p. 132), as Beckett was himself.

More remarkably still, there is much in the *Trilogy* that calls the climate of the Purge to mind. The parallels between the *Trilogy* and the literature and journalism that, from the mid- to late 1940s, increasingly drew widespread public attention to the brutal practices in the Purge prisons have yet to be properly examined, but undoubtedly exist. More generally, the Unnamable inhabits a world where 'you must accuse someone, a culprit is indispensable' (*TR*, p. 415). Here one must look innocent at all costs, like the 'bloodthirsty mob' in *Molloy* with 'white beards and little, almost angel faces' (*TR*, p. 33). The Unnamable sees through this world with shattering lucidity:

> We were foolish to accuse one another, the master me, them, himself, they me, the master, themselves, I them, the master, myself . . . this innocence we have fallen to, it covers everything, all faults, all questions, it puts an end to questions. (*TR*, p. 379)

There are few passages with more resonance in the *Trilogy* as a whole. In less sophisticated vein, Molloy excoriates the 'righteous ones', the 'guardians of the peace', with their 'bawling mouths that never bawl out of season' (*TR*, p. 35). Malone's world is one of pursuits and 'reprisals', haunted by the the threat of being 'hounded' by 'the just' (*TR*, p. 195, 276). Moran links rage with 'the court of assizes' (*TR*, p. 127). The Unnamable associates persecution with an assembly of 'deputies' (*TR*, 315).

It is Molloy, however, who most vividly evokes both the violence and the habit of doublethink that plagued France for at least a decade:

> Morning is the time to hide. They wake up, hale and hearty, their tongues hanging out for order, beauty and justice, baying

for their due. . . . It may begin again in the afternoon, after the
banquet, the celebrations, the congratulations, the orations . . .
the night purge is in the hands of technicians, for the most part.
They do nothing else, the bulk of the population have no part in
it, preferring their warm beds, all things considered. Day is the
time for lynching, for sleep is sacred. (*TR*, p. 67)

Self-evidently, this is not a direct evocation or historical representation. As with the references to the War and the Resistance, however,
what is at stake is not only dispersed images and scattered words and
phrases, but images whose historical content has been displaced,
language whose allusion to historical realities is characteristically
oblique.[27] The obliquity is crucial, as is the sporadic and unreliable
Irishness of the characters, in holding the historical material at a
remove. But the point par excellence, of course, is that history in
the *Trilogy* exists as rubble, as debris strewn across its pages. The
historical deposits in question constitute much of Beckett's imaginative raw material during this period. The *Trilogy* presents us with
a (suitably distant) mode of treating and transmuting them. The
question, finally, is what exactly that treatment involves.

The characters in the *Trilogy* themselves bear many of the
marks – indignity, degradation, shame, suspicion, cruelty, voluntary anaesthesia, a tainted past, a bitter knowledge of repression
and injustice – that had disfigured France after its defeat. So, too,
up to a precisely delimited point, in their rage, their outbursts and
recriminations, their lapses into furious incoherence, they are close
in tone to the atmosphere of post-war France as crystallized, for
example, in the transcripts of the Laval trial. This is above all the
case with *The Unnamable*. The theme of the relationship between
justice and speech looms large in both novel and trial. Unlike the
Unnamable, however, Laval decided not to go on, choosing silence
before the process had ground to its inevitable conclusion. Above
all, the impassioned self-torment in which the characters of the

Trilogy are caught up, their tumultuous, anguished quarrels with themselves, both internalize something of the condition of France itself, and function as a metaphor for and analogy to it.

In all of these respects, the *Trilogy* seems to insist on a cultural temper whose memory de Gaulle, his allies and successors were concerned briskly to expunge. Here Beckett seems very close indeed to Duras, of whom we know he approved.[28] The intransigent anti-heroism of the *Trilogy* represents a fierce repudiation of the ethos of post-1944 Gaullist France, its insistence on renewal and purification, its rewriting of the recent past. If the 'people' in *Molloy* 'so need to be encouraged, in their bitter toil, and to have before their eyes manifestations of strength only, of courage and of joy' (*TR*, 25), neither Molloy nor Beckett himself will pander to that need. Deliberately, and at times derisively, Beckett toys with the language and symbols of the Gaullists. Malone's automatized profession of loyalty is strictly ironical:

> Yes, that's what I like about me, at least one of the things, that I can say, Up the Republic!, for example, or, Sweetheart!, for example, without having to wonder if I should not rather have cut my tongue out, or said something else. Yes, no reflection is needed, before or after, I have only to open my mouth for it to testify to the old story. (*TR*, p. 236)

When Moran whimsically imagines being left trailing 'like a burgess of Calais' by his son (*TR*, p. 129), he is indexing a classic point of reference for heroic French nationalism. It is even not inconceivable that Molloy's object resembling 'a tiny sawing-horse' (*TR*, p. 63) is a trivially distorted, absurdly ironical version of the Cross of Lorraine, ‡, the symbol of Joan of Arc, another such point. After 1944, in a slightly different form, as the symbol of the Free French Forces and the United Resistance Movement, it was visible everywhere in France, from flags to helmets.[29] French humourist

Pierre Dac promised collaborators that, by the time the Purge was ended, they would be 'nothing more than a small heap of garbage'.[30] 'Tout est dit. A la poubelle' (*DI*, p. 131): with the declaration that someone is less than properly human, everything seems said, and one can consign the entity in question to the dustbin. By contrast, Beckett himself stubbornly constitutes his characters as (and sometimes literally in) Dac's heaps. His interest is in human rubbish *per se*, not as the antitype of regenerate man.

The Unnamable, above all, is the character in Beckett's writings in the 1940s who seems most determined to resist the rousing tones of Gaullism, or at least, the specious exhortations to positivity of which Gaullist France no doubt enhanced his sense. The Unnamable hears a lot of stirring talk: 'They have told me, explained to me, described to me, what it all is, what it looks like. And man, the lectures they gave me on man, before they even began trying to assimilate me to him' (*TR*, p. 326). The voices in question want to elevate the Unnamable above itself, to 'decoy' it into a superior 'condition' (*TR*, p. 363). They therefore alternately assure it that 'the big words must out', and 'plaster' it with their bilge or *Quatsch* (*TR*, p. 341). They try to convince it of eternal truths. But there is nothing timeless about these voices. Their grandiosely humanistic rhetoric is historically specific: it was common currency in the smashed cultures of the former belligerents during the first two or three decades of the postwar recovery. This would hardly have surprised Beckett, who thought there was an intimate relation between 'pestilence or Lisbon or a major religious butchery' and the birth of noble sentiments (*DI*, p. 131). The deep Voltairean streak in him is unmistakeable here. His principal experience of the kind of voices with which the Unnamable struggles was through Gaullism. He understood their humanism as a failure of sensibility and intellectual courage. He also knew that they incessantly created or reproduced the very problems they aimed to solve, threatening a return of 'the incriminated scenes' (*TR*, p. 318):

They gave me courses on love, on intelligence, most precious, most precious. They also taught me to count, and even to reason. Some of this rubbish has come in handy on occasions, I don't deny it, on occasions which would never have arisen had they left me in peace. (*TR*, p. 300)

Underlying the mood of 'recovery' was drastic and irreparable loss. Beckett's post-war work is steeped in it. The Unnamable speaks out of an awareness of historical damage not readily to be mended, if at all. Its situation may be irredeemable.

Irredeemable, certainly, in the terms of Charles de Gaulle: the voices want the Unnamable to forget its pain, or be at worst modestly pained. They want it to proclaim its 'fellowship' with them and 'swallow' its 'fellow creatures' in general (*TR*, pp. 300, 327). In the spirit of the times, they want above all to see it *reconciled*. That is, they want it 'loving [its] neighbour and blessed with reason' (*TR*, p. 338). They want it to acknowledge the prevalence of justice and harmony. But the Unnamable adamantly refuses to be dragged out into the light of the true, the good and the right. It is inveterately and invigoratingly hostile to any form of uplift:

Ah but the little murmur of unconsenting man, to murmur what it is their humanity stifles, the little gasp of the condemned to life, rotting in his dungeon garrotted and racked, to gasp what it is to have to celebrate banishment, beware. (*TR*, p. 328)

In this, it is faithful to one of Beckett's deepest inspirations, whilst also repudiating the mode and tone of the historical rescue packages so relentlessly doled out to modern man.

Like Molloy, Moran and Malone, again, the Unnamable is, in its way, a scapegoat, loaded down with a consciousness of the sins that others are anxious to shrug off. If Girard is the great theorist of the scapegoat, its great archivist is Sir James Frazer. In two volumes of *The Golden Bough*, *The Dying God* and, in particular, *The Scapegoat*, above all 4.3, 'The Periodic Expulsion of Evils in a Material Vehicle', Frazer tells us of the attempts made by many communities 'to dismiss at once the accumulated sorrows of a people' by draping figures in the baleful tokens of recent historical evils.[31] Amongst the Iroquois, the men of the village actually went about collecting these tokens. Scapegoats were sometimes holy ascetics, as in the *Jataka*. But they often cut a more melancholy figure than that. The scapegoat could be sick, diseased, debilitated, grotesque or sinful, 'broken down by debauchery'.[32] Certain communities specifically laid 'the painful but necessary duty' on 'some poor devil, some social outcast, some wretch with whom the world had gone hard'.[33] Significantly for the *Trilogy*, men and women might choose the role of scapegoat voluntarily, 'diverting evils threatening others to themselves'.[34]

The characters in the *Trilogy* bear the burden of contemporary history like scapegoats. But as scapegoats, they do not just suffer. Beckett puts them to work. 'How [can we] live without bitterness and without hatred in the vicinity of criminals and traitors, even if they are well locked up?' asked an outraged French correspondent of *La résistance savoyarde* soon after the war.[35] The *Trilogy* responds to this kind of question with a concept of 'living with' that is also one of 'working through'. Beckett had always been interested in the idea of 'continuous purgatorial process' (*DI*, p. 33), associating it with Joyce's treatment of 'the vicious cycle of humanity' (ibid.). The *Trilogy* rejects any quick solution, notably in narrative terms. As a response to contemporary France, it counters purges with purgatorial labour. 'They loaded me down with their trappings', says *The Unnamable*, 'and stoned me through the carnival' (*TR*, p. 327). He calls to mind many *pharmakoi* stoned before him, like Eumolpus in the *Satyricon*. Eumolpus is impoverished, intellectual, inept, 'a tattered thing' and 'cold scarecrow'. He is stoned in the temple for caring about language and 'the loveliest of the arts', and reciting good poetry in an inimical world (in his case, Nero's Rome).[36] The Unnamable's sentence may possibly derive partly from 9 February 1937 in Dresden, where Beckett prudently avoided being out on *Faschingsnacht* (*GD*, 9.2.37). We shall hear more of him stumbling through the postwar carnival shortly.

7

Make Sense Who May:
A World at Cold War, 1950–85

En attendant Godot was first performed in Paris in 1953, at the
Théâtre de Babylone, with Roger Blin as director. Beckett enjoyed
his first major success – as a French playwright. But *Godot* rapidly
attracted a wider audience. It established Beckett's reputation
and made him money. It also turned an author who had been
first Irish, then French into an international figure. In the early
1950s, those who showed interest in his work or sought to promote
it were French or Paris-based. After *Godot*, the names of non-
expatriate Americans begin to loom large in the Beckett story:
Barney Rosset of Grove Press in New York, who became Beckett's
major American publisher; Pamela Mitchell, agent for Harold
Oram over the American rights to *Godot*, who became Beckett's
lover; biographer Richard Ellmann, scouring Europe for facts about
Joyce; director Alan Schneider. Germans started taking an interest,
too. English responses were more mixed. Here, Beckett at first
encountered another version of the rejection he had experienced
before. The *Daily Mail*'s loudly proclaimed view of *Godot*, for
example, was that THE LEFT BANK CAN KEEP IT.[1] Among intellectuals, directors, actors and actresses, however, Beckett always
had his staunch supporters: Harold Hobson, Kenneth Tynan,
Donald Albery, Peter Hall, Donald McWhinnie, Barbara Bray
(a lover over many years) and, later, Billie Whitelaw, John Calder
and Harold Pinter. In a drearily philistine culture deeply distrust-
ful of intellect, they defied both censors and populists alike. They

En attendant Godot, Paris, 1961.

were all the more valuable to Beckett in that, appalled by Irish censorship, for a while, he imposed a ban on all performances of his plays in Ireland.

Thus Beckett's name started featuring in a larger world. It would do so ever more diversely, not least as a result of the emergence of the academic Beckett industry. The explosion of Beckett studies ensured his global currency, if sometimes principally as a distinctively French luminary (an existentialist, *nouveau romancier* or dramatist of 'the absurd'). Beckett the man also began to circulate in a larger world. He had always gone back and forth quite regularly between France and Ireland. At the time of the attacks on *Godot*, in terms reminiscent of *Murphy*, he had despaired of the 'shopkeepers', as he called the English.[2] Nonetheless, like many an Irish genius before him, he started to need them. England now became crucial as an outlet for his work in English (or his translations of his own work in French), and he spent increasing amounts of time in London, directing or advising on productions of his plays, not least those he wrote for radio and, later, television.

He also spent more time in Germany, for similar reasons. He went to the United States only once, to help produce *Film*, where he was snubbed by an American genius, Buster Keaton, the star who played the central role, and came away feeling that 'this is somehow not the right country for me . . . the people are too strange'.[3] But if Beckett stayed away from America, American scholars increasingly came to him. Indeed, academics from all over the world visited him, sent him books, essays and manuscripts and besieged him with queries and requests for work. Theatrical colleagues from abroad paid frequent visits. Beckett

Beckett at a rehearsal of *En attendant Godot*.

clearly felt a profound kinship with some of them, notably the driven, alcoholic, magnificently expressive Irish actors Jack McGowran and Patrick Magee. Old friends and family members frequently appeared in Paris, as did individuals whom Beckett turned into personal causes, like the ex-San Quentin lifer Rick Cluchey.[4]

This side of the later life of a man often regarded as one of the great exponents of modern solitude – in the *German Diaries*, Beckett had evoked '[t]he absurd beauty of being alone'[5] – can look rather frenetic and even inconsequential. Hectic Beckett seems anomalous. But it is equally odd to assume that the two sides of Beckett's life were not connected. A weird, symbiotic, late twentieth-century logic insistently closed the gap between him and world. On the one side, contemporary culture was awestruck by someone it took to be so refractory to its order. It idolized the anchorite and busily sought to drag him from his lair. It battened on him in proportion to its reverence for his incorruptibility, and begged him for more of his art whilst making ever larger incursions into the time he needed to produce it. It expressed its devotion in contradictory and almost ruinous forms. His fastidiousness and distaste for publicity were loudly blazoned abroad. On the other side, Beckett's exquisitely scrupulous disposition allowed the world to sweep him up, not least, into the most extraordinarily painstaking practical work for the theatre, whilst he repeatedly deplored the futility of his absorption. *Faute de mieux*, he adopted the tactics of the modern double life. The conditions for the 'siege in the room' had receded into the past. In order to be able to continue to write, he spent more time in what, since 1953, had been his second home, the little house that he and Suzanne had had built near Ussy-sur-Marne, 'recuperat[ing] something in the silence and solitude'.[6] He fed off all these complications, but they were also a source of pathos. He produced a great deal of extraordinarily innovative and curious, beautiful work, but his relationship with Suzanne dried up. He allowed the

'The anchorite
dragged from his
lair': Beckett, 1956.

demands of others and his highly developed sense of responsibility towards them to torment and exhaust him, leaving him with
'dreams of deserts'.[7] He was often enervated by much of the activity
he engaged in.

The later Beckett occasionally reverts to one or other of his
former writing selves, conspicuously in the case of the play *All That
Fall* (1957), one of his most Irish works. Remarkably, however, just
as, from the late 1930s, Beckett evolved from an Irish into a French

writer, so from the mid-1950s, he adapted not only himself but his art to a new historical situation, and evolved into an international one. This development had two main consequences. On the one hand, a truly abstract Beckett finally emerged. The kind of historical residue perceptible in the earlier work tends to fade from the great prose work of the period, *How It Is* (1964), and the more formal works and 'cylinder pieces' of the late 1960s and early '70s: *Imagination Dead Imagine, Ping, Enough, Lessness, The Lost Ones*.

At the same time, however, from the mid-1950s onwards, there is a strain in Beckett's art which seems less abstract than global. The works in question are fraught with the recognition that something has happened to history itself. They clearly respond to a historical condition, that of the Cold War – or at least, to particular phases of it – which seemed all-encompassing as none had been before. The connection between historical context, life and art, however, was by no means as rarefied as it might seem. The focus of the Cold War, after all, was on the European theatre, particularly Berlin. It was notably in Berlin that, from 1945 onwards, West and East confronted each other. Khrushchev called the city 'the testicles of the West'. 'Every time I want to make the West scream', he explained, 'I just squeeze on Berlin'.[8] Beckett no doubt heard the scream. Berlin was a city which he repeatedly visited and grew to know well. If he became a Berliner during the Cold War, however irregularly, it was no accident.

The impact of the Cold War on Beckett produced, above all, the great play *Endgame* (*Fin de partie*). *Endgame* was composed between 1954 and 1956. The years 1953–62 saw a major escalation of the Cold War and the beginning of nuclear crisis. The USA developed and tested its first version of the H-bomb in 1952. The Soviet Union followed suit in 1953. In the words of the *Times*, 'the most portentous, and certainly loudest, event of 1954 occurred not in Washington or London or Moscow but on a desolate coral reef in the Pacific, 2000 miles north-east of Australia. The explosion of a hydrogen bomb at

Fin de partie (the French version of *Endgame*), Paris, 1957.

Bikini in March . . . dwarfed the Hiroshima bomb, and physicists were quick to add that there appeared to be no theoretical limit to the size of such bombs'. From now on, man would be haunted by 'the vague spectre of "universal death"'.[9] The test was the first in a series 'which only served to heighten international anxiety'.[10] US Secretary of State John Foster Dulles quickly asserted that the US must rely on nuclear weapons rather than conventional weaponry. By 1954, he was advocating the doctrine of 'massive retaliation' to any act of Soviet aggression.[11]

Since the Soviet Union was capable of similar retaliation, this logically led to the bleak certainty of MAD, mutual assured destruction. The North Atlantic military alliance, NATO, had come into force in 1949. In response, on 14 May 1955, the Communist states signed the Warsaw Pact Treaty, according to which members pledged to defend each other if attacked. Two vast armed power blocs now eye-balled each other malevolently across the Iron Curtain. The abortive Hungarian revolution of 1956, in which the Hungarians rose up against their Soviet-imposed government only promptly to be suppressed by armed invasion, clearly underlined the division. When, during the Suez crisis of the same year, the US sought to curtail Soviet threats in the Middle East, 'massive retaliation' became a practical threat. Dulles introduced the concept of brinkmanship, famously declaring that 'the ability to get to the verge without getting into the war is the necessary art.'[12] Henceforth, it seemed, the world would have to live according to a MAD rationale, in a state of more or less muted terror of the end.

Literature, theatre and the arts were quick to respond imaginatively to this scenario. In Orwell's *1984* (1949), the condition of Oceania is post-atomic. In J. B. Priestley's *Summer Day's Dream* (1949), a few paltry survivors of a nuclear holocaust succeed in building a better way of life.[13] In Ray Bradbury's *Fahrenheit 451* (1953), a book-burning dystopia is consumed by nuclear war. The boys in William Golding's *Lord of The Flies* (1954) flee a nuclear attack. The melancholy of the post-apocalyptic vision reached its peak in 1957, with Nevil Shute's *On the Beach* locating the scattered remnants of humanity in Australia, forlornly awaiting death by fallout. In the cinema, Arch Oboler scripted and directed *Five*, America's first film about nuclear survivors, in 1951. Other such films followed: *Invasion USA* (1952), *The Day the World Ended* (1955) and *World Without End* (1958). The desolate landscape sporadically indicated in *Endgame* is intimately related to such settings, seems as comprehensively devastated as many of them do, and shares their shocked, contaminated air. Jack MacGowran recalled that, for the 1964 production at the English Theatre in Paris, Beckett shortened the descriptions of what Clov sees outside the windows because he 'wanted to leave a doubt' about any continuance of 'the existence of human life'.[14] Early reviews of *Endgame* on both sides of the Atlantic Ocean were printed on pages surrounded by fearful news of the nuclear arms race.

Of course, by now, it is possible to reflect on the plaintive historicity of the threat of Armageddon, the fugitive experience of the end of the world drawn near, with something akin to astonishment. But the fear of wipe-out was extremely serious, and extremely grim. There was certainly a strain in Beckett's disposition which was intimate from the start with the Cold War ethos. The thought of prodigious cataclysm is undoubtedly what fuels the appalled hilarity of *Endgame*. So, too, we get the measure of the integrity and candour of the play if we set it alongside the machinations of the cultural Cold War, which implicated writers as diverse as Koestler, Spender, Malraux, Trilling, Arendt and even Orwell, to name but a few, and ensured, for example, that the extraordinarily successful British literary journal *Encounter* was bankrolled by secret subsidies from the CIA. In the classic, sobering and highly instructive account of the theme, Frances Stonor Sanders's *Who Paid the Piper?: The CIA and the Cultural Cold War*, there is no mention of Beckett.[15]

Historicity is nonetheless a crucial matter in *Endgame*. For it is the historicity and therefore the avoidability of the historical end itself that the play urges upon us, by insisting that we view it from alternative or conflicting perspectives. The play appears to address a general condition. In the world according to *Endgame*, the 'farce' is the same, 'day after day' (*CDW*, p. 106). The time is always 'the same as usual' (*CDW*, p. 94, 109). But equally, when Hamm declares that 'it's the end of a day like any other day' (*CDW*, p. 98), this cannot strictly be the case at all, since he declares it in a world where there is no longer tide or Turkish delight, where there are no more bicycles or 'paupers' to be 'inspected' (*CDW*, p. 96), lights cannot come on in the evening, the survival of rats is implausible and it is not conceivable that anything could be visible 'on the horizon' (*CDW*, p. 107). Indeed, in this particular world, 'there's no more nature' (at least, 'in the vicinity', *CDW*, p. 97); or rather, nature exists only in Clov's richly ironical sense: other people, like the 'old doctor' and Mother Pegg, have 'naturally' died. Mother Pegg's light has 'naturally' been extinguished (*CDW*, p. 104, 112). One thing is clear: 'outside of here it's death' (*CDW*, p. 96). 'The whole place stinks of corpses' (*CDW*,

p. 114). Humanity is apparently doomed to extinction; though alas, says Hamm, in great perturbation, it might start 'all over again' from a flea (*CDW*, p. 108).

Thus *Endgame* presents us with a paradoxical world in which 'time was never and time is over' (*CDW*, p. 133). Its 'universals' seem alternately to exist beyond historical specifics, and to be determined by them. The Cold War scenario appears to disappear, then reappear. This was literally the case with productions of the play. When Beckett himself directed it at the Schiller Theater in Berlin in 1967, the set suggested a fallout shelter or bunker.[16] Yet he objected to Douglas Stein's post-apocalyptic set for Harvard's American Repertory Theatre production in 1984. So, too, in the play itself, the post-nuclear scenario looms large or recedes according to how far vestiges of other historical contexts make themselves felt. There are moments, for example, when Beckett appears to be thinking once more of the historical endgame of the Anglo-Irish gentry, the last, grey phase of their decline. Beckett's *Theatrical Notebooks* suggest that he also had the First World War in mind.[17] This is understandable. He wrote *Endgame* not long after he acquired his 'little house in the "Marne mud"'.[18] Seine-et-Marne, which included Ussy, had been at the centre of the two Battles of the Marne in 1914 and 1918. Ussy was one of seven towns within twelve kilometres to be awarded the French Croix de Guerre 1914–18 for its sangfroid and powers of endurance. It was a Beckettian place. The desolate images that the area called to mind also edge their way into *Endgame*.

The split between historical markers and ahistorical claims is definitive of *Endgame*, and one of two cardinal features that appear throughout it. The second is the split between a little world and a big one.[19] The play alternately blames one and the other for its characters' afflictions. This, too, breaks up any impression of a grandly final vision of things. If devastation appears to have swept across the landscape, it is Clov, says Hamm, who 'pollute[s] the air' (*CDW*, p. 93). Since Adorno, critics of the play have emphasized how far it implies and is concerned with a political macrocosm.[20] But it also wilfully diminishes the importance of any larger view. The principal representatives of humanity in the play are two oddballs who bicker over matters like the ribbon on a three-legged black toy dog. The historical specificity of the play provokes the very universalizing abstractions it also resists. Weirdly, absurdly, unpredictably, the laughable, mean little staged actuality of *Endgame* constantly tells us that it is part of a whole, yet obstinately refuses to be absorbed into one. As Hamm and Clov are patently inadequate to their predicament, so, too, one level of the play is inadequate to the other. In a world where equilibrium, strategic thinking, a seemingly boundless hi-tech competence, what Adorno called instrumental reason had all come to spell MAD, Beckett insisted on constructing a profoundly wonky play in which the elements simply don't hang together. As for human history: strangely, on occasions by a hairsbreadth, at length, in one of its historical phases, humanity was eventually to assert itself, at least, in so far as it determined one particular limit to its inhumanity. In doing so, nearly thirty years after *Endgame* was first performed, it bore out Beckett's statement of faith.

By the late 1960s, nuclear armament had got the Soviet Union into economic trouble, and the Vietnam War had thrust America into crisis. The certainty of MAD had become a balance of power. Meanwhile, West Germany had adopted a policy of *Ostpolitik*, seeking to normalise its relations with the Eastern European nations, including East Germany. The first Strategic Arms Limitation Treaty (SALT) talks took place in June 1972. In 1975, these were followed by the Helsinki Accords on security and co-operation in Europe. Predictably, tensions relaxed. But the mood of *détente* did not last long. Ronald Reagan became American president in January 1981, and promptly vowed to increase military spending and to oppose Communism across the globe. A new

Anglo-American axis (Reagan and British Prime Minister Margaret Thatcher) denounced the Soviet Union in the old ideological terms. Thus began what some historians now call the New Cold War (1979–85). Reagan announced his Strategic Defence Initiative or 'Star Wars'. For its part, the Soviet Union entered the 1980s with the largest thermonuclear arsenal in the world, and a stock-pile of medium-range missiles primed to annihilate Europe briskly if necessary.

But there were important differences between the New Cold War and the old one. Reagan and Thatcher's Cold War manifested itself in a flurry of localized conflicts. In 1983, for example, the US intervened in the civil war in Lebanon and invaded Grenada whilst also involved in counter-revolutionary activities in Nicaragua – all this in a year that Reagan baptized the 'Year of the Bible'. Mean-while, the Soviet Union was engaged in a war in Afghanistan and increasingly disposed to intervene in the Middle East, Africa and Asia. The Communist bloc was also energetically repressing its more awkward and troublesome citizens. In Czechoslovakia, the Charter 77 group struggled with the totalitarian regime for civil rights. The regime responded by arresting and interrogating the Charter signatories, not least writers. In Poland in 1980, the inde-pendent trade union Solidarity provoked the government into declaring martial law and curtailing political freedoms. Solidarity remained a beleaguered and clandestine organization until the late 1980s. Meanwhile, the East German government was persecuting, arresting, imprisoning and deporting dissident writers like Wolf Biermann and Rudolf Bahro.

The second major difference between the 1950s and the early 1980s was that, in the West, the dominant forms of thought about the Cold War had changed. This was partly the consequence of America's involvement in the Vietnam War, which had made people much more sceptical about Cold War rhetoric, and often radicalized them. What the Cold War historians call revisionism exemplifies the shift. Historians during and after the Vietnam War were far more likely to raise awkward questions about Western demonizations of Communism than they had been before it; to suspect the us of imperial ambitions, a will to global hegemony and economic domination of Europe; to consider the two sides in the Cold War as mirror-images of each other; and to wonder whether its hidden dividends were not in fact domestic, the control and discipline of mass populations and the dogged maintenance of two inherently unstable ideologies.[21]

These were precisely the conditions in which Beckett produced his gaunt, off-centre allegories of the early eighties, *Quad* (1981), *Catastrophe* (1982) and the last play he wrote, *What Where* (1983). These plays are precisely connected to their historical context. Beckett had always been concerned about the freedom of writers, a concern that no doubt stemmed initially from his distaste for Irish and English censorship, and later from his experience of the more drastic Nazi and Vichy versions of it. He was drawn to prisoners, an interest that, from time to time, was reciprocated by prisoners or ex-prisoners themselves. He had long been troubled by the idea of incarceration (though it is by no means clear that he separated political incarceration from other forms, as self-evidently in a moral class of its own). From the apartment in the Boulevard Saint-Jacques that he and Suzanne took over in 1960, he could see the Santé prison, and was reputedly in the habit of communicating by mirror with one of the inmates. He took the side of playwright Fernando Arrabal when he was imprisoned by the Franco government, and of opponents of the French use of torture during the Algerian war. He boycotted racist South Africa.

More specifically, Beckett waived royalty payments on productions of his plays in Eastern Europe. He supported an appeal against the proclamation of martial law in Poland. He also supported and encouraged the young Polish writer and translator Antoni Libera. Libera told Beckett about the precursor of Solidarity, the Committee for the Defence of Workers, and Beckett subsequently had his Polish royalties paid to Libera, who used them to support writers and publishers who were at odds with the regime. He even hoped to assist Libera in escaping Poland. In the case of Czechoslovakia, his principal concern was Václav Havel. Havel was a Czech dramatist who had been banned from the theatre since the Prague Spring in 1968. In the terms of the regime, at least, the publication of the Charter 77 manifesto declared him to be a traitor and a renegade. He was placed under surveillance, subjected to house arrest, then thrown into prison. The International Association for the Defence of Artists invited Beckett to write a piece on Havel's behalf. Beckett agreed. The result was *Catastrophe*. In Germany, Beckett espoused no particular cause. Yet in West Berlin, he repeatedly directed or contributed to productions of his own plays just a few miles away from the Berlin Wall. It is hardly likely that he was unconscious of the significance of doing so.

Catastrophe at the Barbican Pit, London, 2006.

Catastrophe expresses one of Beckett's responses to the era of the New Cold War. It reeks of distaste, at once principled and aesthetic, for the crass, indifferent language of power in operation. 'Step on it, I have a caucus . . . Get going! Get going! . . . Good. There's our catastrophe. In the bag. Once more and I'm off . . . Now . . . let 'em have it' (*CDW*, pp. 458–60): whilst the officious and dictatorial D. (the Director) issues his instructions, P. (the Protagonist) remains frozen, immobile, '*head bowed*', speechless, '*inert*' (*CDW*, pp. 457–61). Finally, however, he '*raises his head*' in defiance (*CDW*, p. 461). Beckett stated that the point of *Catastrophe* was clear and precise. When a reviewer said the end of the play was ambiguous, he reacted angrily: 'There's no ambiguity there at all . . . He's saying, you bastards, you haven't finished me yet!'.[22]

No ambiguity, indeed: like its Protagonist, *Catastrophe* is stubbornly recalcitrant. But it is also ironically devised. What Beckett claims P. is 'saying' obviously relates to Havel and the plight of political prisoners in Eastern Europe. But the play itself has nothing directly to do with that plight. P. may or may not be an image of it; but in *Catastrophe* itself, he is chiefly D.'s victim, and D. speaks the language of the Western boardroom, ministerial office, management suite or military command. Furthermore, D. has another victim, A., his Assistant, an underling and a woman. The substantial concern of the play is power relations in the Western workplace, and crucially includes the exploitation of women. At the same time, the workplace in question is also specific, a theatre; D. is a theatre director; and P. is both a representation of oppression, and oppressed himself. When he '*fixes the audience*' at the end (*CDW*, p. 461), P. even invites it to contemplate its own implication in the structures of power that the play has described.

Without its ironical structure, *Catastrophe* might lead a sceptic to wonder whether, after all, Beckett could not have featured in *Who Paid the Piper?*, if only fleetingly. From the late 1970s, the US had increasingly focussed on human rights movements as part of its continuing drive to victory over Communism. The CIA had sought to foment dissidence in the Communist bloc, and bankrolled cultural activities that appeared to encourage it. By using theatre to address the human rights issue in Eastern Europe from outside it, albeit innocently, Beckett might appear to coincide with US covert operations. Inconveniently for such an argument, however, *Catastrophe* seems to be telling the West to look to its own abuses of power. In fact, the play conflates two political criticisms. It is indeed unambiguous, but because it turns in both directions with such rigorously lucid detachment. Beckett was almost constitutionally devoid of self-righteousness. By the same token, he was nothing if not expert in the serpentine ways of complicity. It is one of his great themes, perhaps almost his greatest. Like the revisionist historians who were working in the same period, he understood the logic of the Cold War as that of the Moebius strip. In *Catastrophe*, he addressed a Communist abuse of power obliquely, through an image of a Western one. In doing so, he also insisted on a principle of reversibility endemic to the Cold War itself.

The Protagonist in *Catastrophe* raises his head. It is at least a gesture of minimal revolt. In *Quad* and *What Where*, the faint kindling of resistance gutters and then dies. Indeed, both *Quad* and *What Where* might have been called *Catastrophe*, with different but increasingly stark implications. In *Quad*, four figures pace a strictly delimited space in regular rhythm, repeating the same courses and procedures, which require them to avoid each other. The enclosed space calls prison-yards to mind, but also West Berlin, at that time another gaol-space, and one within whose confines Beckett walked a great deal. In *Quad*, all boundaries and limits are in principle unbreachable. All conditions have been specified from the start. Beckett's directions insist on lockdown. The area is 'given . . . Four possible solos all given. Six possible duos all given . . . Four possible trios all given . . . All possible light combinations given . . . All possible percussion combinations given

... All possible costume combinations given' (*CDW*, pp. 451–52). The situation in *Quad* is that of Vladimir and Estragon as specified in one of Beckett's terse notes on *Godot*: 'From outset no help'.[23] *Quad* renders this situation in an abstract, mechano-balletic form.

Quad is about imprisonment, and emerges partly from Beckett's political concerns at the time. It is also about imprisonment in a structure. The structure at stake is scarily Janus-faced. There are two quads in *Quad*: the main square and an inner one, marked E in a second diagram in the directions (*CDW*, p. 453), towards which the figures converge and from which they diverge. E is the locus in which the figures may become entangled, graze each other or collide, where mishap may occur, where the structure may wobble or collapse, the process go wrong. Here *Quad* allows for a minimal sense of possibility, a hypothetical (but material) point at which an otherwise entirely binding logic may founder. Since the directions specifically tell us that E must be 'supposed a danger zone' (ibid.), however, the point at which the structure may break down is also the site of menace and possible disaster. Paradoxically, *Quad* turns out to be about risk, and even brinkmanship.

In *What Where*, by contrast, there is not even the slightest hint of an alternative to the closure it depicts. One after another, four men tell of giving others 'the works' (*CDW*, pp. 472–76); of making them scream, weep and beg for mercy; but also of failing to extort a necessary confession from them. Having confessed to failure themselves, they exit, to become one of those 'worked on' in their turn. A phantom figure designated simply as V – he tells us he is a fifth personage, though his voice belongs to one of the four – presides over this grisly scenario. V is dramaturge, technician, critic, chief observer, *deus ex machina* and a discourse inhabiting the others, all at once. The structure of the play is almost ritualistic. As such, it leads towards V's stony conclusion that, though 'time passes', the form of its passing is unrelenting, and unrelentingly reproduces and reinforces the operations of power: 'In the end

I appear. /Reappear' (*CDW*, p. 476). By the same token, in the
closing lines, the last lines Beckett ever wrote for a theatrical
public, as in *Catastrophe,* he decisively repeated the lessons of the
Cold War, in repudiating all ideological justifications of the naked
exercise of power without scruple, whatever their partisanship:

> Make sense who may.
> I switch off. (*CDW*, p. 476)

Yet one of the nicest ironies in Beckett's work is that, in his last
and perhaps his most disquieting play, by dint of an extremely
precise choice of words, if only theoretically and *sotto voce*, he
is able to indicate a connection between abandoning the habit
of self-vindication intrinsic to 'making sense', and disabling
the machines of modern terror.

8

Where He Happened To Be:
Capital *Triumphans*, 1985–9

The gloom of *What Where* might have seemed appropriate enough
in 1983, the climax of a little period that, from 1979, seemed to
promise the resurgence of a brutal international politics. By 1986,
however, as far at least as the Cold War was concerned, matters
wore a different complexion. In 1985, Mikhail Gorbachev came
to power in the Soviet Union. The Soviet economy was heading
for disaster. Gorbachev saw this, and sought to turn it in a different
direction. His policy of *perestroika* directed funds away from military
and towards civilian uses. The *glasnost* that accompanied it meant
that the Communist regimes became more open and transparent,
and admitted the justice of criticism from within. The Soviet bloc
increasingly brought the abuses that *Catastrophe* and *What Where*
had partly addressed to a halt.

Reagan and Thatcher scented justification and ideological
victory, not least because the West was experiencing an economic
boom. Reagan agreed to scale down the arms race, and, in a series
of summits ending in Moscow in 1988, both sides drastically
reduced their nuclear arsenal. By the late 1980s, a new breed
of what Beckett had called the 'hardened optimists' (*MU*, p. 157) –
brusquely self-cauterizing, impatient to forget the wounds of
the world – were talking of the emergence of a 'new world order'.
The term first appeared in 1988. In 1989, Francis Fukuyama
published an essay entitled 'The End of History?', anticipating
his book of 1992, *The End of History and the Last Man*, in which

'His era was over':
Beckett in Paris,
late in life.

he argued that humanity had arrived at the *telos* of its evolution
as exemplified in Western democratic societies.[1] Shortly after
the essay appeared, Beckett died.

It was as though he knew that the era that had shaped him
and determined the character of his art was over. However, he
would certainly not have responded to the concept of 'the end of
history' with anything other than hawk-eyed scepticism. So much
is clear from that great work of his final years, *Stirrings Still* (1988):

> So on unknowing and no end in sight. Unknowing and what
> is more no wish to know nor indeed any wish of any kind nor

therefore any sorrow save that he would have wished the strokes to cease and the cries for good and was sorry they did not. (*csp*, p. 263)

Just a month before his death, the Berlin Wall, of which he had been conscious for so long, finally came down. By then, Beckett's own particular corner of the new world order was Le Tiers Temps, an old people's home. Rather than rejoicing with the optimists, or indeed, celebrating at all, he appeared to be acutely anxious. Having watched some television footage from Berlin in his room, 'he emerged very agitated' and exclaimed to the *directrice*, Madame Jernand, '*Ça va trop vite*'.[2] It is a luminous moment. To attribute Beckett's 'agitation' simply to debility finally unstringing the nerves would be to diminish him. He had always nursed a sage and clear-eyed distrust of any solution 'clapped on problem like a snuffer on a candle' (*di*, p. 92).[3] '*Ça va trop vite*' had formed part of his injunction to Ireland in the 1930s, and to France and the world immediately after the war.

'They loaded me down with their trappings and stoned me through the carnival' (*tr*, p. 327): Beckett did not survive to witness most of the developments after Gorbachev conceded victory to the Western way of life. There are few if any less Beckettian spectacles than the eudemonistic carnival of triumphant Capital – the champagne culture – that followed the end of the Cold War (at least, as far as 2008). It is hard to imagine him fitting in. Or is it? The irony in the Unnamable's remark is very delicately judged. As a writer who claimed to have breathed deep of the vivifying air of failure all his life, Beckett hardly understood self-satisfaction. He was a faster not a feaster, as Coetzee says of Naipaul, in a modern world which offered 'less and less of a home to the fasting temperament'.[4] Yet, as he grew older, his *modus vivendi* was by no means radically at odds with post-war European, affluent middle-class norms. True, he told Barney Rosset in 1958 that he wanted to 'put a stop to all

this fucking *élan acquis* and get back down to the bottom of all
the hills again, grimmer hills than in '45 of cherished memory'.
He was, he feared, in danger of finding himself 'entangled in pro-
fessionalism and self-exploitation'.[5] Nonetheless, in many respects,
he bore the 'trappings' of his success sedately if not comfortably.

Indeed, given that he intensely disliked celebrity – he shunned
publicity, turned down most of the honorary degrees he was offered
and, when he was awarded the Nobel Prize in 1969, did not attend
– he might even seem to be an example of what Fukuyama called
the 'last man', short on *thymos*, the will to win recognition, but
much concerned with inconspicuous self-preservation. Knowlson
comprehensively demonstrates how far the later Beckett was caught
up in and reconciled to a conventional and even stolid version of
the lifestyle of the post-war bourgeois professional. He had two
residences, city and country, and discussed his commuting arrangements with friends. He quarrelled with others over building rights
on neighbouring land. He was weighed down with correspondence,
made and kept endless appointments, took jet flights and argued
over contracts. In the rapidly consumerizing 1950s, he acquired the
usual spoils: car, television, telephone. He had separate telephones
for business and private life. He planted trees in his garden at Ussy,
worried about the state of his lawn, took long recreational walks
and listened to sport and classical music concerts on the radio. He
married Suzanne. But they also led increasingly separate lives, and
Beckett had affairs. He developed particular tastes in food and drink
and worried about his heating and his addictions to alcohol and
tobacco. He was sometimes worn out by rush and bother, and
took holidays in sunny places, increasingly for reasons of health.

'Histoire banale', as he said of *Play*,[6] a work which, in its own
fashion, is about modern life, or at least, modern adultery. There
are two key aspects of the later Beckett, however, which run counter
to this description of him. The first, of course, is his later writing,
which explores zones of experience and sensibility quite beyond

the usual horizons of middle-class life, and posits a concept of 'last men' (and women) extremely remote from Fukuyama's thesis. The second is his attitude to money and possessions. During his time in London, Beckett had lent Tom MacGreevy money, at the same time urging him that there should 'never be any talk of debts and loans and all the other lousinesses of give and take *entre ennemis* between us. When it's there it's there and when it's not it's not and *basta*'.[7] This was to prove characteristic of him. He was an admirably, casually, prolifically and almost alarmingly generous man. He gave spontaneously, with no thought of getting back. He was seemingly quite indifferent to what Marx called exchange value and Murphy thinks of as the rule of the *quid pro quo*. It was a feature he shared with some of his contemporaries at the École Normale, who were mindful of the *normalien* code of heedlessness of self. Sartre, for example, had little or no interest in creature comforts, did not have a bank account and gave money away to friends throughout his life.[8]

Thus when Ethna MacCarthy fell ill, Beckett offered to help her with money 'up to the limit'.[9] He waived all fees for Rick Cluchey's production of *Endgame*, and gave money to Cluchey and his family. He gave away the Jack Yeats painting he owned and loved (to Jack MacGowran). He paid the tax bill of his friends the Haydens, helped the MacGowran family when Jack died, and paid money into the trust fund for the children of Jean-Marie Serreau, a man he did not like, just as, years earlier, in Germany, he had made the acquaintance of Arnold Mrowietz, a part-time tailor who repelled him, and then ordered a suit from him. He supported the insignificant young writer Jean Demélier, and bought him 'an entire wardrobe'.[10] He frequently gave cash to charities and family members. He paid for friends' holidays. He gave away his Nobel prize money (to some very good causes, like B. S. Johnson and Djuna Barnes). At the same time, he himself showed a 'total lack of interest in any kind of luxury or display',[11] and his apartment and house in Ussy were furnished with

Spartan simplicity. He was even remarkably cavalier about parking fines. Cronin tells a fine story of Beckett's kindness to two porters from Dublin's National Gallery who decided to holiday in Paris. (He took them everywhere from the Louvre to a brothel in Montparnasse.)[12] But if one story particularly illustrates Beckett's disdain for 'give and take *entre ennemis*', it is Claude Jamet's account of the night when a tramp approached him in a Montparnasse bar and complimented him on his jacket. Beckett promptly took the jacket off and gave it to him. 'Without emptying the pockets either'.[13]

Put Beckett's profligacy together with his minimalism, the wilful self-destitutions of his art, and it might seem logical to conclude that his aesthetic is levelling, and even egalitarian. He insisted, after all, on the fact and the importance of 'being without', in more senses than one (*DI*, p. 143). He stated that 'my own way was in impoverishment' and spoke of his 'desire to make myself still poorer'.[14] He dreamt, he said, 'of an art unresentful of its insuperable indigence' (*DI*, p. 141). Troublesomely, however, he seems dismissive of egalitarians themselves. Take, for example, his satirical account of the political agitator in *The End*:

> He was bellowing so loud that snatches of his discourse reached my ears. Union . . . brothers . . . Marx . . . Capital . . . bread and butter . . . love. It was all so much Greek to me. (*CSP*, p. 94)

'He had a nice face', adds the narrator, 'a little on the red side' (*CSP*, p. 95); but this abrupt cluck of liking hardly encourages more respect for the man's views. That Beckett worked a deliberate reference to the 'Marx Cork Bath Mat Manufactory' (*MU*, p. 46), whose existence he had noted in London, into *Murphy* confirms the impression of a detachment from political radicalism that bordered on flippancy, and even derision.

Still more problematically, Steven Connor has shown that the difficulty with reading Beckett in terms of economics is that, in his work, less keeps on turning out to mean more. On the surface of things, Beckett's 'poetics of poverty' reflects a determination 'to resist not only the values of the commodity and the market-place, but the value of value itself'. Alas, however, negativity itself insidiously keeps metamorphosing 'into different varieties of positive value'.[15] Publishing houses, the institutions of the performing arts and academic scholarship and criticism all unceasingly convert Beckettian minimalism into profit. The Beckett industry has become one of the largest and most distinctive multinational corporations in the literary world. Furthermore, with *Worstward Ho* as his example, Connor shows how far Beckett himself was aware of this problem of recuperation, and dramatized and explored the necessity of living with the reversibility, not only of value, but of non-value into value, of diminished resources into increase.

Connor's argument is incontrovertible, the more so because he sees *Worstward Ho* as finally exploring ways in which the double-bind in question might be resisted if not cancelled out. Rather than trying to wobble along the same tightrope, I'd suggest that another element also needs to be introduced into the equation which, if it does not allay the irony on which Connor insists, makes its bonds less harsh. The point is best demonstrated if we turn from money to that quintessential feature of the culture that surrounded the later Beckett, consumerism. No one who knows anything about Beckett would expect his writings to be crammed with references to consumer durables. In this respect, his work appears to occupy the opposite end of the aesthetic spectrum to, say, Bret Easton Ellis's *American Psycho* – which, though it first appeared only two years after his death, belonged to a different world to Beckett's, and is another token of the end of his era – thus expressing its austere elevation above historical particulars.

Yet, at the same time, many Beckett texts include a brand name or two. More strikingly still, the consumer items in question are often notably significant and even precious to the narrator or character concerned. In *Waiting for Godot*, for example, Pozzo is dismayed by the loss of his 'Kapp and Peterson' (*CDW*, p. 35). The reference is to a select manufacturer of tobacco pipes in Dublin, and has the interesting effect of making Pozzo seem much more clearly Irish than he does elsewhere. In *Molloy*, Moran congratulates himself 'as usual on the resilience of my Wilton' (*TR*, p. 109). Beckett clearly knew that Wilton carpets were supposed to last: they had long been associated with good wear and advertised accordingly. The Unnamable speaks of rubbing itself with 'Elliman's Embrocation' (*TR*, p. 323), though this well-known contemporary remedy for a variety of physical aches and pains seems unlikely to be much use for some of its more outlandish afflictions, like lack of limbs. In *Endgame*, Clov supplies Nagg with a 'Spratt's medium' (*CDW*, p. 97), thus treating him like an animal (since the reference is to a popular English dog biscuit) but also quite a classy one (since Spratt's were originally associated with the English country gentry). Coincidentally, Spratt's was playing out its own endgame at the time, and closed down not long after the play was first performed.

A pretension to class, or at least gentility, seems very much at stake in some of Beckett's references to products. His narrators and characters often speak of the most humdrum consumables as if they were savouring exotic delicacies or lifting fine wines to the light. But other pretensions may also be on show. When Murphy and Ticklepenny contemplate the question of warming Murphy's garret, for instance, the narrator behaves as though he has suddenly become a heating expert, interjecting that 'It seems strange that neither of them thought of an oilstove, say a small Valor Perfection' (*MU*, p. 94). The connoisseur and the specialist come together in Beckett's choicest consumerist allusion: in *Molloy*, Moran promises himself 'to procure a packet of thermogene wool, with the pretty demon on the outside' (*TR*, p. 139). Thermogene wool was supposed to warm the body and cure coughs, rheumatisms, chest ailments and pains in the side. The reference to the demon places the product in question as specifically the French *Le thermogène*, not Beecham's Thermogene Wool. Beckett's taste is unerring: it was indeed a pretty demon, with very nice legs. The Thermogene demon was the invention of Leonetto Cappiello, whose innovative and often beautiful advertising posters were sufficiently well-known for him to have achieved canonical status by the 1940s.

Indeed, so pretty was Cappiello's demon that it actually figured in not just one but two great post-war novels. George Perec's *Life: A User's Manual* refers to 'boxes of thermogene wool with the fire-spitting devil drawn by Cappiello'.[16] But this makes the image seem

Leonetto Cappiello's 'pretty demon' in an advertisement for *Thermogène* wool.

fiercer and less sexy. It also lacks the sense of Moran's discernment. Beckett's oddballs, tramps, vagabonds, destitutes and down-and-outs turn out to be remarkably pernickety about consumer goods. When they talk about them, they sound like fastidious aesthetes; this in striking contrast to their lack of discrimination in other spheres of their lives, whether gross or despairing. If products appear only rarely in Beckett's works, his narrators and characters like to convey the impression that that is because they can take them or leave them. Beckett himself occasionally replicates this attitude with a loftiness that is all his own. In *Molloy*, for example, Moran and Gaber drink Wallenstein's lager. This sounds plausible enough to be real, and Beckett's *German Diaries* show a considerable knowledge of kinds of German beer. But these do not include Wallenstein; not surprisingly, because no such beer existed. Beckett got the name from Schiller's (not very funny) trilogy *Wallenstein*, the first part of which is called *Wallensteins Lager*, meaning Wallenstein's Camp.

Beckett's insertions of consumer items are invariably playful. They sound a little like what (in the *German Diaries*) he called 'precise placings of preposterous *Tatsachen* [facts]'.[17] But the irony involved is by no means footling. On the one hand, the allusions suggest a limited but necessary resignation to the historical world in which he lived: after all, as Molloy so justly remarks, 'you cannot go on buying the same thing forever . . . there are other needs, than that of rotting in peace' (*TR*, p. 75). Indeed, he even goes so far as to consider combining meditational and commercial practices: 'If I go on long enough calling that my life, I'll end up by believing it. It's the principle of advertising' (*TR*, p. 53). This, of course, is as ludicrous an idea as the Unnamable's momentary supposition that it might smother in 'the crush and bustle of a bargain sale' (*TR*, p. 294). In all three cases, nonetheless, the character's ironical tone wryly acknowledges his historical situatedness. On the other hand, from Murphy onwards, even in the direst straits, Beckett's characters display a reverse (or perverse) version of the aristo-cratic *hauteur* which, however impoverished, refuses to grant any significant status to the world of commerce. However profound one's forlornness – or so the argument apparently goes – there are certain depths to which one does not sink.

Murphy quotes Arnold Geulincx: '*Ubi nihil vales, ibi nihil velis*': 'Where you are worth nothing, want nothing' (*mu*, p. 101). From time to time, consumer items may come Beckett's characters' way, and please them. But his characters do not want them, in Geulincx's sense. They do not hunger for them, or insatiably pursue them. 'And things,' asks the Unnamable, 'what is the correct attitude to adopt towards things? And, to begin with, are they necessary?' Strictly speaking, no: 'if a thing turns up', it tells itself, 'for some reason or another, take it into consideration'. But finally, 'People with things, people without things, things without people, what does it matter' (*tr*, p. 294). When it's there it's there and when it's not it's not: Beckett knew very well that the culture of advanced capital was no more capable of expressing a whole than cash was likely to stay in the hand. The conviction of the contingency and historicity of that culture generates some robust shoulder-shrugging. Both he and his characters give the impression of being quite simply indiffer-ent; indifferent to the imperatives of capitalism, indifferent to the politics that opposes it. This was equally the case in life and art. In his very last sentence, Molloy decides that 'Molloy could stay, where he happened to be' (*tr*, p. 91). Beckett clearly learnt this, too. He presents the culture of advanced capital as where he hap-pens to be, like a wanderer who, one evening, finds he has strayed on to a not entirely featureless but not very interesting plateau.

This, however, is less true of Beckett's writings in the eighties than it is of his earlier work. As Capital announced its imminent triumph, Beckett held it at an even greater distance. As it promised to fill every space and make every void substantial, his work ever more insistently emptied the world out, becoming more and more phantasmal and wraith-ridden. Where so many of the dominant discourses of the decade were raspingly ugly and assertive, Beckett's work was poignantly shot through with strains of an exquisite, poignant gentleness, with 'patience till the one true end of time and grief and self' (*CSP*, p. 261). *Ohio Impromptu* (1981), *Ill Seen Ill Said* (1982), *Nacht und Träume* (1984), *Stirrings Still* (1988): these works brought to fruition an aspect of Beckett's artistic practice beginning with '. . . *but the clouds* . . .' (1976). They remain rooted in the familiar Beckettian profession of unknowing, as in the case of the figure in *Stirrings Still*,

> resigned to not knowing where he was or how he got there or where he was going or how to get back or to whence he knew not how he came. (*CSP*, p. 263)

The tone, however, is subtly different to that of similar moments in earlier works. In Beckett's last writings, not knowing becomes, not only an instance of the desolation of self, but also inextricable from sadness for others. He was partly fulfilling an obligation he had enjoined upon himself almost fifty years previously, when, in an entry in the *German Diaries* (*GD*, 4.1.37), he had exhorted himself to *Zärtlichkeit* not *Leidenschaft*, the use of tenderness, not passion.

Of course, none of this comes easy. But the note of compassion is the stronger for having to fight its way through other and more familiar Beckettian idioms. Thus, in *Ill Seen Ill Said*, the usual wrestle with language, the poverty of language, the insufficient poverty of language – 'Resume the – what is the word? What the wrong word?' – resolves itself by cracking open:

> Riveted to some detail in the desert the eye fills with tears. Imagination at wit's end spreads its sad wings . . . Tears. Last example the flagstone before her door that by dint by dint her little weight has grooved. Tears. (*IS*, p. 17)

'And here he named the dear name': *Ohio Impromptu* at the Barbican Pit, London, 2006.

At the same time, almost for the first time, serious images of comfort in suffering appear in Beckett's work. In the wordless *Nacht und Träume* (a play for television), two hands appear, successively offering drink to a painfully solitary figure, wiping his brow and resting gently on his head, as though in benediction. Most hauntingly of all, *Ohio Impromptu* tells the story of a man who, having lost a 'dear face', quits the residence they had shared for another, then recognizes too late that he cannot return, since 'Nothing he had ever done alone could ever be undone. By him alone' (*CDW*, p. 446). In this extremity 'his old terror of night' lays hold on him. Then succour arrives:

> One night as he sat trembling head in hands from head to foot
> a man appeared to him and said, I have been sent by – and here
> he named the dear name – to comfort you. Then drawing a worn
> volume from the pocket of his long black coat he sat and read
> till dawn. Then disappeared without a word. (*CDW*, p. 447)

As so often, Beckett speaks by piling up obstacles. Even the tone of this short passage is not immune to an insidious tonal ambivalence (particularly in the little play on 'head in hands' and 'head to foot'). The mood of the play almost collapses under the weight of its distancing devices (the story is not enacted, but itself narrated by one figure to another. The listener repeatedly interrupts it with knocks on the table. The two figures have curious, identical appearances, with long black coats and long white hair). Nonetheless, an extraordinary consolatory language glints in the dark. Its power is inseparable from its melancholy:

> So the sad tale a last time told they sat on as though turned to stone. Through the single window dawn shed no light. From the street no sound of reawakening. Or was it that buried in who knows what thoughts they paid no heed? To light of day. To sound of reawakening. What thoughts who knows. Thoughts, no, not thoughts. Profounds of mind. Buried in who knows what profounds of mind. Of mindlessness. Whither no light can reach. No sound. So sat on as though turned to stone. The sad tale a last time told. (CDW, p. 448)

Fleetingly, here and there, insistently if intermittently, the late Beckett breathes a new, secular life into a concept that, as his last works themselves tell us, has come to seem virtually inarticulable: *misericordia*.

It is hard to imagine references to the culture of consumption in *Ohio Impromptu*. But the attitude to possessions perceptible in Beckett's late writings is nonetheless an extension or extreme version of his earlier attitude. Money and consumer items feature here and there in Beckett's work, much as do animals, vegetables and philosophers, and are casually treasured or (on occasions) lightly passed over in the same way. This points in two directions. Even as Beckett settles for the world of advanced capital as where he 'happens to be', however minimally, whatever the moments of collusion, he also holds open another space for thought to those that characterized the dominant ideologies of his era. This is what Simon Critchley means when he writes of Beckett's 'weak messianic power'.[18] Beckett is scrupulous, almost beyond comparison, in his repudiation of suspect positivities. He is adamantine in his refusal to conspire 'with all extant meanness and finally with the destructive principle' (to quote Adorno).[19] He therefore chooses a *via negativa*. If 'the task of thinking is to keep open the slightest difference between things as they are and things as they might otherwise be', then that task is supremely exemplified in Beckett.[20] As Connor says of *Worstward Ho*, Beckett will not surrender the idea of another sphere or possibility of value, however apparently absurd, minimal or purely negative its form. This negative space is the space of art; or rather, Beckett takes the preservation of the negative space to be integral to art's task.

Thus a historical life of Beckett, even when it is as shrunkenly conceived as this one, logically requires an epilogue that turns its focus on historically specific forms of human life inside out. That is what my last little chapter tries to do.

Afterword: To Begin Yet Again

The current intellectual scene is perplexing. Vitalisms, cognitivisms, fundamentalisms; theologies new-born and old-revived; slight and possibly even fatal pragmatisms, presentisms and populisms: all these flourish gaily, as items in the contemporary market of ideas. They are options with as much and as little significance as any other range of choices available to a contemporary consumer. Or, to put the point differently: we cling to them like shards of detritus after a great shipwreck. Living 'in the wake' is what matters. The twentieth century arrived at a previously unimaginably sophisticated conception and grasp of history that appeared to be connected to and in some degree hold out an august political promise. Yet, paradoxically, the century of historicism pursued to an extraordinarily subtle extreme also turned out to be one of profound historical catastrophe. As Giorgio Agamben tirelessly insists, it is delusional to suppose that we are in the process of extricating ourselves from this paradox. The ghosts of the last century are not to be exorcised by isolating particular and localized features of its unfolding horror, or seeking to cleanse our consciousness of it by treating specific 'traumas'. That is merely to replicate (if in suitably updated terms) the blithe progressivism that Beckett dismissed out of hand. The last century is not behind but before us, as a conundrum we have yet to learn to contemplate, let alone solve. In this respect, the culture might study Beckett's art of 'slow going' very thoughtfully.[1]

In his life and art, Beckett spanned the larger part of the twenti-eth century. Like other great writers who have come to fame since 1945 – Celan, Coetzee, Sebald – he was haunted by the paradox I have described. According to this paradox, the evidential truth of history is philosophically implausible, and vice versa. There is no philosophical logic to the assumption of a world comprehen-sively deprived of a greater good, *a priori* and *ab ovo*; except insofar as that assumption seems everywhere borne out by history. Beckett wrote in a world become obscure, because it was impossible to trust either in history, or in any possibility of transcending history. He was clearly tempted by a kind of secular Manichaeanism, a philo-sophical position singularly appropriate to modern history, and one to which recent French philosophers, from the late Sartre (in the *Critique of Dialectical Reason*) to Badiou, Jambet and Lardreau have sometimes edged close.

Beckett lived through or witnessed the devastating upheavals in Ireland of the 1920s, the indifferent callousness of modern English imperialism and mercantilism, the political and cultural violence of National Socialism in Germany, the dire injustices of the Vichy regime, the Purge and the early years of the Fourth Republic in France, the terrors of the Cold War and the evolving triumph (and self-congratulation) of Western Capital. He saw everything he needed to see to supply him with a logic for historical revulsion. The world he knew was that of the historical remainder, unregenerate, unillumined historical experience, history as issueless maze, an indefinite prolif-eration of blind alleys. The roots of this knowledge, of course, were Irish. The history of Ireland presented a seven- or eight-hundred-year-old narrative of frequently brutish colonialism. To those who inherited the legacy of colonial Ireland, history itself could all too easily seem like a labyrinth to be negotiated only with great difficulty, from which there was no certainty of any release. Joyce's Stephen Dedalus was one such heir. Joyce himself was another, if in a differ-ent way. The early Beckett bears some startling resemblances to

Stephen in *Ulysses*. But as a young Dublin Catholic intellectual whose culture will soon be in the ascendant in Ireland, Stephen Dedalus knows both that history is his nightmare, and that he must struggle to awake from it. As a young Protestant whose culture was in its death throes, Beckett was deprived of any such knowledge and assurance. As for making good: he and his class were deprived of any thought of atoning for the past – whatever that might mean – long before they might conceivably have begun to deem it necessary.

Thus Beckett can only abstract from history, since it will never properly be his. Hence the fact that, whilst his work lacks historical density, others have repeatedly thought of it as very much about historical experience. But if history remains an abstraction for him, he is also condemned to bear it as an eternal millstone round his neck. The young Beckett was emphatically the obverse of Joyce's Englishman Haines, to whom Stephen sends a telegram quoting Meredith: '*The sentimentalist is he who would enjoy without incurring the immense debtorship for a thing done*'.[2] For Beckett, who had a horror of sentimentality, a New Year could only be 'a new turn of the old screw'.[3] History unfolds as a seemingly unending endgame. The problem is ontological: history is stymied by what Beckett calls 'the authentic weakness of being'. It is inert, with the inertia of infinite differentiation, and is therefore powerless to save itself. 'If you really get down to the disaster', Beckett added, 'the slightest eloquence becomes unbearable'.[4] The weakness of being chokes language at its point of utterance, makes words seem both futile and *de trop*.

Hence the coexistence of two crucial aspects of Beckett's work that I have emphasized here: *melancholia* and *misericordia*. *Melancholia* arises from Vladimir's conviction that there is 'nothing to be done' (which seems partly to be a tart rejoinder to Lenin's great historical question of 1902).[5] The later Beckett increasingly responds that there is nothing to be done; and yet . . . *Misericordia* assumes that one cannot remain indifferent to the plight of others astray in

'Misericordia': Beckett in 1961.

the labyrinth. A third aspect of Beckett and his work which I have not emphasized very much, largely because others have, is *caritas*, goodness to others. This is more relevant to Beckett than the concept of the 'good friend'. In one sense, obviously, he was a very good friend indeed, but it is not wholly clear that he ever properly experienced friendship, if friendship means intimacy; at least, to judge by the immense gulf that repeatedly yawns between others' accounts of him and his own writings, the sense of lives lived in different worlds. In Beckett, *caritas* was a function of *melancholia* and *misericordia*. The three together are clearly expressions of a uniquely receptive sensibility. One cannot doubt accounts of Beckett's extreme sensitivity to the pain and distress of others, or Barbara Bray's description of him as 'hyperaesthetic'.[6]

The trouble with my three terms together is that they are in danger of making Beckett sound like a Christian stoic, which he certainly was not. They form part of a resiliently secular structure of thought. But what most decisively saves Beckett both from mere stoicism, Christian or other, and from secular manichaeanism, insofar as he is saved, is a conviction of the possibility of the event, in Alain Badiou's sense and definition of that term. Philosophically, the event is a haphazard occurrence of that which appears for the first time, whose emergence is not foreseeable and which cannot be described according to prior laws of causality. From the Copernican transformation of our conception of the universe to the French Revolution, from the love affair that can redefine an ordinary life to Picasso's modernist experiments in painting, events appear as decisive breaks with the given. They are supplements to what we have previously taken for the world. However fleetingly, the world is made new through events. Apart from them, it exists as a remainder. The term remainder designates history shorn of events and their consequences. It is the world as inhabited by Vladimir and Estragon in *Waiting for Godot*.

Most of the major traditions in Beckett scholarship have tended immediately to pitch themselves at a certain level of abstraction, whether philosophical or modernist. They assume that abstraction is self-evidently commensurate with Beckett's work. However, a new positivism has recently been invading Beckett studies. Its consequences have sometimes been invigorating. In the end, however, particularly if its orientation is historical, positivism does not logically end in an anti-philosophical account of Beckett. It rather explains why philosophical thought, or an activity akin to it, was essential to him. Philosophical and theoretically-based readings of Beckett in general repeatedly accomplish one side of his project, or confirm it in place. For they reiterate and extend his insistence on the privilege of the speculative intellect relative to historical disaster.

But there are two ways of thinking of Beckettian abstraction, abstraction as retreat from the historical process, and abstraction as intervention in it. Marjorie Perloff and Pascale Casanova have both suggested that a certain kind of (initially French) abstraction from Beckett has long been determined by a headlong flight before the shockwaves of modern history. This was first of all the case with a generation of French intellectuals who wrote on him soon after the war: Bataille, Nadeau, Mayoux, Blanchot.[7] Here, again, it is important that the 'Paxtonian revolution' be comprehensively factored into Beckett studies. In their differing ways, the intellectuals had reason to feel at least embarrassed and at times distinctly if not extremely uneasy about recent French history. Not surprisingly, they gave special place to a non-French (and ex-Resistance) French writer, whilst also rarefying his texts. Like the Gaullists, Bataille and Blanchot were concerned to sever connections with a recent history to which they felt uncomfortably close.[8] They had a positive interest in not thinking Beckett historically.

This particular mode of abstraction then fed into and subsequently underpinned a whole tradition of first French and then Anglo-American post-structuralist abstraction in Beckett studies. The result was a great deal of fascinating and sometimes brilliant work, but work whose abstraction remained cloistered, whose horizons were strictly those of the very academic milieu Beckett deserted, and which repeatedly confirmed the ahistorical principle in Beckett studies. Badiou's philosophy also writes history off. But it does so by way of slicing directly across history, thinking history from the vantage point of its possible transformation. His thought of the event annuls history in the interests of other possible histories, histories told by futures beyond our grasp, histories made available to those who are nothing as yet, who exist at the level of 'heaps of garbage'. Beckett thinks in very similar fashion in 'Saint-Lô'. Badiou shares Beckett's double insistence: if it is crucial to register the pervasive trace of history, it is also crucial to negate it.

Badiou conceives of events as taking place only rarely. In this respect, whilst very much against the current grain, his thought is exactly appropriate to Beckett. If the possibility of the event is rare in Badiou's philosophy, it is so rare in Beckett as to be almost imperceptible. Beckett was captive to a hyper-scrupulous conviction of the extreme difficulty of thinking the event, a difficulty amply borne in on him by recent history. He dedicated himself to that conviction because he knew that its logic was imperious. For Beckett as for Badiou, there is nothing 'behind' the world. Nothing decrees that the world must be or stay as it is. What we think we are and know is founded on nothing. The supposition that the world can be made new is therefore logical. Nothing disputes it; except history, which everywhere disputes it. If one paradox is intrinsic to Beckett's works, it is that of the predicament from which there is apparently no exit, but which is also groundless. One may wait interminably for Godot. There may never be any evidence that he will make himself manifest, or indeed that he exists. But there is nonetheless no reason to suppose that the order of the world definitively excludes the possibility of his arrival. In a sense, the whole of Beckett's project consists of a mimicry of history, in that it endlessly piles up obstacles to the idea of the transformative event. Ironically, however, as in

Quad, the space of possibility can never be absolutely closed down, and thus the project reverses: the more Beckett seems determined to throttle the idea of the event, the more he actually preserves it or demonstrates that it is unkillable. This is the profound if contorted reasoning underlying his well-known assertion that the key word in his plays is perhaps.[9]

Thus, strange as it may seem, Bersani and Dutoit are right when they argue that Beckett is committed to producing 'formulas for starting again'.[10] His will to write off the world is not to be separated from this commitment. Beckett asserted that 'Art loves leaps' ('L'art adore les sauts', *DI*, p. 128). He throws this in the teeth of Leibniz. According to Leibniz, *natura non facit saltus*, nature makes no leaps: this is the depressingly inexorable principle of natural continuity. Beckett himself appears to adhere to it when, at the beginning of *Murphy*, he states that 'The sun shone, having no alternative, on the nothing new' (*MU*, p. 5). But art can break this iron law and serve as a paradigm for breaking it. This is why Beckett could say that his work was 'about' the disappearance of the world.[11] He claimed to 'think in new dimensions', and told Charles Juliet that the only possible affirmation was to 'give form to the unformed', the yet-to-be-formed.[12]

Vivian Mercier once claimed that Beckett felt that 'the entire human experiment has been a failure and must not be repeated'.[13] Many of Beckett's works come close to saying this. But this does not mean that he imagined that the 'human experiment' thus far was the only one possible, or even that he imagined it that it was the only one possible to human beings. The truly inveterate Beckettian repudiation is of the backward look: hence his distaste for naturalist and realist aesthetics, which are always founded on it. Hence also his disdain for empiricism: he has no investment whatever in a concept of knowledge as rooted in experience. '[My] work does not depend on experience,' he told Lawrence Harvey, 'it is not a record of experience'.[14] In this respect, his modernism might seem opposed above all to Humean modernity; were it not for the fact that, as Hume himself makes clear in the *Treatise on Human Nature* 1.3, if knowledge derives only from experience, then that exactly defines its generic limits, and categorically distinguishes its scope, procedures and relation to the world from those (for example) of the prophetic, anticipatory, speculative (and therefore denunciatory) powers of the imagination. In this respect, Beckett is actually a late descendant of Hume, and his work continues to spread the modern scare inaugurated by Hume, who terrified many of his contemporaries.

To repudiate the backward look, however, is not to rid oneself of history. Indeed, it is to run all too large a risk of being overpowered by it again. If, as I have suggested, Beckett's art is purgatorial and the figure of the scapegoat is central to it, that is because his art is caught up in a work of historical ridding or voiding. Thus, in 'Saint-Lô', Beckett assists the 'old mind' to 'sink into its havoc', in the interests of 'other shadows' that have yet to be born into their own 'bright ways' (*CP*, p. 32). Yet, at the same time, even as he seeks to write it off, he also partly identifies the old mind as his own. It is thus that he prepares the ground for others. Whatever the sometimes considerable merits of more recent discourses on Beckett and technology, textuality or the body, their good cheer is initially made possible by a feature of Beckett's work that is quite distinct from those they focus on. Like Joyce, Beckett assumed 'the holy office': 'Myself unto myself will give/This name, Katharsis-Purgative'. Beckett's work functions partly as a historical conduit, bearing off what Joyce called the 'filthy streams' that obstruct others' dreams.[15]

As this Life has tried to show throughout, Beckett's art twisted and turned with vicissitude, with the historical situations in which he found himself. Yet he also displayed great tenacity and singleness of purpose, what he called an 'aversion to half-measures and frills'.[16] This showed in various different ways. It appeared in his work for the Resistance and the Irish Red Cross and his acute sense of responsibility to friends and family members. It appeared in his ferocious powers of concentration. It was even evident in his way of bicycling, 'panting up the hills in bottom gear, refusing to give in, like my father'.[17] But above all, it showed in his attitude to his art: in his battles with censorship; in the intensity and precision of his demands as a director of his own plays, which were sometimes more than his actors and actresses could bear; in the flat and unequivocal manner in which he turned down requests from others – directors, producers, publishers, prize awarders – if they appeared to require that he compromise his integrity, or that of his work.

For all the ruse of its title, the odd one out of the chapters in this book, the one which places Beckett in relation, not to a more or less profoundly disquieting set of historical circumstances, but to an enabling one, is the chapter on the École Normale. *Normaliens* have repeatedly demonstrated an acute grasp of Beckett's sense of

'A romanticism *bémolisé*, flattened, as B is flattened to B flat': Caspar David Friedrich's *Two Men Contemplating the Moon*.

the fluidities of mind and world. But they have also noted that it co-exists with its obverse, a recognition that at a certain point, if only in exceptional circumstances, it is crucial that one determine a limit to infinite recession. This is not surprising, because the same emphasis is repeatedly present in the work of *normaliens* themselves, as one might expect from an institution that produced Bourbaki and Lautman along with Herr. By yet another paradoxical twist of logic, absolute uncertainty and the imperative of Proust's 'granite point' turn out to be twin sides of the same coin. At a certain moment in the indefinite flow of the world, one chooses to stick and become unbudgeable, because nothing will otherwise decree any point at which it is necessary to do so. As Václav Havel put it, Beckett understood that, if one were not to prove 'indifferent to the run of things', one would occasionally have to take 'the meaning of affliction' upon oneself.[18]

Beckett's sticking-point has finally a double aspect. He takes extremely, awesomely seriously the Romantic doctrine that, in Matthew Arnold's words, art is a criticism of life. He literalizes it, radicalizes it, pursues it intransigently and all the way down, takes it quite beyond any conception of which Arnold was capable, to the point where he almost produces a parody of it. He transmutes it into an extravagantly negative and sometimes violent aesthetic. He also rudely strips it of the self-gratifying nobility and humanistic dignity to which the Romantics and their successors remained in thrall. In the *German Diaries*, he at one point suggests that the only romanticism 'still tolerable' for us is, like Caspar David Friedrich's, *bémolisé*, flattened, as B is flattened to B flat.[19] At the same time, he persists in whilst also radicalizing and demystifying the Romantic and post-Romantic conviction of the possibility of a secular grace, the occasion, experience, chance, epiphany or trajectory which transforms our understanding of what life can be. To say that he makes this conviction difficult and virtually unsustainable is an understatement. Yet it flickers here and there in his work, flaring unpredictably where we might least expect it, as in *Worstward Ho*, which abruptly introduces a word that has a specific weight in Romantic discourses, joy:

> No mind and words? Even such words. So enough still. Just enough still to joy. Joy! Just enough still to joy that only they. Only! (*WH*, p. 29)

In the context of Beckett's work as a whole, that the narrator himself should seem confounded by the appearance of the word is fitting enough. But the possibility of a moment like this is intrinsic to Beckettian failure and impotence. For, though every epoch is vigorously intent on promoting its own instruments of historical closure, be they hadron colliders, race science, economism, the victory of the proletariat, empires, God or DNA, nothing can quite stop history springing extraordinary surprises for the good on us, however intermittently or rarely; nor entirely smother our own capacity to respond to them.

References

Introduction: Fuck Life

1 In his famous ninth thesis on the philosophy of history. See Walter Benjamin, 'Theses on the Philosophy of History', *Illuminations*, ed. and intro. Hannah Arendt, trans. Harry Zohn (London, 1979), pp. 255–66 (p. 260).

2 The first quotation is from Edward Moerike's *Mozart on the Way to Prague*, trans. Walter and Catherine Alison Philips (Oxford, 1934), which Beckett is reviewing.

3 James Knowlson, *Damned to Fame: The Life of Samuel Beckett* (London, 1996), p. 19. Knowlson refers to 'the fledgling biographer I was in 1989' in 'Samuel Beckett: The Intricate Web of Life and Work', *Journal of Beckett Studies*, xvi/1–2 (Fall 2006/Summer 2007), pp. 17–29 (p. 17).

4 Knowlson, *Damned to Fame*, p. 19.

5 See Louis Aragon et al., eds, *Authors Take Sides on the Spanish War* (London, 1937), p. 6.

6 See Jean-Paul Sartre, 'Merleau-Ponty vivant', *Les Temps Modernes*, xvii/84–5 (1961), pp. 304–76; and Georges Canguilhem, *Vie et mort de Jean Cavaillès* (Ambialet, 1976).

7 *Beckett and Badiou: The Pathos of Intermittency* (Oxford, 2006).

8 See Steven Connor, *Samuel Beckett: Repetition, Theory and Text* (Oxford, 1988), pp. 190–97.

9 'The essential thing is not knowing whether one is right or wrong, that really has no importance. What is necessary is to discourage the world from paying one much attention . . . The rest is vice'. Louis-Ferdinand Céline, *Mort à crédit* (Pléiade, *Romans*, vol. i; Paris, 1981), p. 688; quoted *GD* 1.10.36.

10 In 'The Waste Land'. See T. S. Eliot, *Collected Poems* (London, 1939), p. 72.

11 For a more extensive account of the battle, see Lois Gordon, *The World of Samuel Beckett 1906–1946* (New Haven and London, 1996), pp. 195–8.

12 More specifically still, to spoliation or pillage, not simply devastation. Havoc! was originally a war-cry or command.

13 One or two critics have looked at particular phases of Beckett's development in this way, notably Marjorie Perloff, in '"In Love with Hiding": Samuel Beckett's War', *Iowa Review*, XXXV/2 (2005), pp. 76–103. Gordon partly covers similar ground to mine in *The World of Samuel Beckett*, but the present study does not stop at 1946; draws on different and sometimes more recent historical research; constantly reads back and forth between historical contexts and Beckett's works; and seeks to locate historical consciousness in their relation.

14 *GD*, 15.1.37; quoted Knowlson, *Damned to Fame*, pp. 244–5.

15 Beckett is quoting Joyce, *Finnegans Wake* (London, 1999), 1.3, p. 49.

16 See David Cunningham, 'Jacques Derrida: Obituary Symposium 1930–2004', *Radical Philosophy*, CXXIX (January–February 2005), accessed at www.radicalphilosophy.com.

1 Arriving at an End: Ireland, 1906–28

1 See James Knowlson, *Damned to Fame: The Life of Samuel Beckett* (London, 1996), p. 6; and Anthony Cronin, *Samuel Beckett: The Last Modernist* (London, 1996), pp. 3–4.

2 As Cronin warns us, *Samuel Beckett*, p. 10.

3 Ibid., p. 10.

4 Quoted John Banville, *The Painful Comedy of Samuel Beckett,* review of Cronin, *Samuel Beckett*, Lois Gordon, *The World of Samuel Beckett 1906–1946* (New Haven and London, 1996), and Knowlson, *Damned to Fame, New York Review of Books*, 14 November 1996; available at www.samuel-beckett.net/banville.html.

5 Quoted at www.portoraroyal.co.uk/portal.aspx/history.

6 R. F. Foster, *Modern Ireland: 1600–1972* (London, 1989), p. 498.

7 The phrase is Knowlson's. See *Damned to Fame*, p. 46.

8 Beckett recounted the story in conversation with Knowlson. See

Damned to Fame, p. 78, and Knowlson's note, p. 720, n. 52.

9 See Clare Hutton, 'Joyce, the Library Episode and the Institutions of Revivalism', in *Joyce, Ireland, Britain*, ed. Andrew Gibson and Len Platt (Gainesville, FL, 2006), pp. 122–38 (p. 135). If Catholics had been statutorily enabled to attend Trinity since 1794, religious tests remained in place until 1873. In the early twentieth century, only not particularly devout Catholics from established, privileged and affluent backgrounds went to Trinity. The institution was seen as 'thoroughly Protestant in government' and teaching 'Protestantism to Protestants'. See Thomas J. Morrissey SJ, *Towards a National University: William Delany SJ (1835–1924): An Era of Initiative in Irish Education* (Dublin, 1983), p. 185. Not surprisingly, perhaps, the Roman Catholic Church itself refused to permit Catholics to study there until 1971.

10 From Gerald Griffin, *The Wild Geese: Pen Portraits of Irish Exiles*; quoted Richard Ellmann, *James Joyce* (revd edn, Oxford, 1982), p. 58.

11 Cronin, *Samuel Beckett*, p. 59.

12 The Act may be accessed at www.irishstatutebook.ie/1923/en/act/pub.

13 The quotation is from the *Irish Vigilance Association*, February 1922. See Ronan Fanning, *Independent Ireland* (Dublin, 1983), p. 57.

14 Cronin, *Samuel Beckett*, p. 36.

15 Lionel Fleming, *Head or Harp* (London, 1965), p. 104.

16 Niall Rudd, *Pale Green, Light Orange: A Portrait of Bourgeois Ireland 1930–1950* (Dublin, 1994), p. 28. Unsurprisingly, it is not hard to find references to Houyhnhnms and Yahoos in the Irish Protestant writings of the period. See for instance Terence de Vere White, *A Fretful Midge* (London, 1957), p. 2.

17 Brian Inglis, *West Briton* (London, 1962), p. 12.

18 See Fleming, *Head or Harp*, p. 33; and Cronin, *Samuel Beckett*, p. 26.

19 Inglis, *West Briton*, p. 12.

20 Ibid., p. 27.

21 Ibid., p. 29.

22 See ibid., pp. 53, 199.

23 De Vere White, *A Fretful Midge*, p. 2.

24 *Mutatis mutandis*, a similar case can be made regarding the work of J. B. Yeats, much beloved of Beckett.

25 Beckett to Alan Schneider, quoted Cronin, *Samuel Beckett*, p. 26.

26 Unsourced quotation, ibid., p. 14.

27 The Vandeleurs' maid: de Vere White's real name was Bernard
Vandeleur. De Vere White, *A Fretful Midge*, p. 11.
28 Lennox Robinson, *The Big House: Four Scenes in its Life* (London, 1928),
p. 60.
29 Though he attended performances of at least two of Robinson's plays.
See Vivian Mercier, *Beckett/Beckett* (New York, 1979), p. 23.
30 Inglis, *West Briton*, p. 22.

2 Not Worth Tuppence: Paris and the École Normale Supérieure, 1928–30

1 Suheil Badi Bushrui and Bernard Benstock, eds, *James Joyce: An International Perspective: Centenary Essays in Honour of the Late Sir Desmond Cochrane*, with a message from Samuel Beckett and a fore-word by Richard Ellmann (Gerrards Cross, 1982), p. vii.
2 See for instance Lois Gordon, *The World of Samuel Beckett 1906–1946* (New Haven and London, 1996), chap. 2 (pp. 32–52).
3 This was the title of McAlmon's autobiography. See *Being Geniuses Together*, revd with supplementary chapters and an afterword by Kay Boyle (New York, 1968).
4 Unsourced quotation, Nicole Masson, *L'École Normale Supérieure: Les chemins de la liberté* (Paris, 1994), p. 12.
5 Barante, *Histoire de la Convention Nationale* (6 vols, Paris, 1851–3), VI, p. 78; quoted A. J. Ladd, *École Normale Supérieure: An Historical Sketch* (Grand Forks, ND, 1907), p. 14.
6 Unsourced quotation, Ladd, *École Normale Supérieure*, p. 33.
7 Robert J. Smith, *The École Normale Supérieure and the Third Republic* (Albany, NY, 1982), p. 16.
8 In *Littérature* (Paris, 1941); quoted Masson, *L'École Normale Supérieure*, p. 73.
9 For an account of this life, see for example Robert Brasillach, *Before the War*, trans. and ed. Peter Tame (Lewiston, NY, 2002), pp. 80 ff.
10 Masson, *L'École Normale Supérieure*, p. 50.
11 See Michael Scriven, *Paul Nizan: Communist Novelist* (London, 1988), pp. 20–22.
12 Alain Peyrefitte, *Rue d'Ulm: Chroniques de la vie normalienne*

(Paris, 1963), p. 334.

13 See ibid., p. 343.

14 See Françoise Proust, *Point de passage* (Paris, 1994), pp. 25–6.

15 Smith, *The École Normale Supérieure and the Third Republic*, p. 131.

16 On which see Diane Rubenstein, *What's Left? The École Normale and the Right* (Madison, WI, 1990).

17 Brasillach, *Before the War*, p. 61.

18 The phrase is Canguilhem's. See Georges Canguilhem, *Vie et mort de Jean Cavaillès* (Ambialet, 1976), p. 17.

19 See Peyrefitte, *Rue d'Ulm*, p. 15.

20 See Daniel Thomas Primozic, *On Merleau-Ponty* (Belmont, CA, 2001), p. 2.

21 Ronald Hayman, *Writing Against: A Biography of Sartre* (London, 1986), p. 74.

22 See James Knowlson, *Damned to Fame: The Life of Samuel Beckett* (London, 1996), p. 218.

23 This evokes a world in which '"each portion of matter may be conceived of as a garden full of plants, or as a pond full of fish", and where, moreover, "each branch of the plant, each limb of the animal, each drop of its humours is in its turn such a garden or pond"'. See Nicholas Rescher, *G. W. Leibniz's Monadology: An Edition for Students* (London, 1991), p. 26; and *DFMW*, p. 47. For a *normalien*'s use of the passage, see Alain Badiou, *L'Être et l'événement* (Paris, 1988), p. 349.

24 See Rubenstein, *What's Left?*, p. 88.

25 Knowlson, *Damned to Fame*, p. 125.

26 See Knowlson, *Damned to Fame*, p. 122.

27 Feldman, *Beckett's Books: A Cultural History of Beckett's 'Interwar Notes'* (London, 2006), p. 47. According to Feldman, Beaufret's copy of L. Debricon's *Descartes: Choix de textes* (Fontenay-aux-Roses, 1892) was in Beckett's library at his death.

28 Smith, *The École Normale Supérieure and the Third Republic*, p. 77.

29 See Hayman, pp. 53–4, 60, 63.

30 Smith, *The École Normale Supérieure and the Third Republic*, p. 78.

31 Feldman, *Beckett's Books*, p. 48.

32 Ibid., p. 45.

33 See Jacques Rancière, *Le philosophe et ses pauvres* (Paris, 1983), pp. 7–8.

34 Lawrence E. Harvey, *Samuel Beckett: Poet and Critic* (Princeton, NJ,

1970), pp. 8–66.

35 'Idées fortement enchaînées'. Charles Adam and Paul Tannery, *Œuvres de Descartes*, 12 vols (Paris, 1897–1910), XII, *Vie et œuvres de Descartes* [by Adam], p. 559.

3 The Ruthless Cunning of the Sane: London, 1933–5

1 Letter to Thomas MacGreevy, undated [late Sept., 1930]; quoted James Knowlson, *Damned to Fame: The Life of Samuel Beckett* (London, 1996), p. 120.

2 Beckett repeated this statement. Quoted ibid., p. 126.

3 J. H. Whyte, *Church and State in Modern Ireland 1923–70* (Dublin, 1971), p. 61.

4 The quotation is from one of his Senate speeches. See Donald R. Pearce, *The Senate Speeches of W. B. Yeats* (Bloomington, IN, 1960), p. 92.

5 'We were the last romantics – chose for theme/Traditional sanctity and loveliness'. W. B. Yeats, 'Coole Park and Ballylee', *Poems*, ed. A. N. Jeffares, with an appendix by Warwick Gould (London, 1989), p. 360.

6 Donald Harman Akenson, *The Irish Diaspora: A Primer* (Toronto, 1993), p. 51.

7 Graham Davis, 'The Irish in Britain 1815–1939', in *The Irish Diaspora*, ed. Andy Bielenberg (Harlow, 2000), pp. 19–36 (p. 32).

8 Ultan Crowley, *The Men Who Built Britain: A History of the Irish Navvy* (Dublin, 2001), p. 132.

9 I am grateful to Ronan McDonald for raising this question with me. See also n. 19.

10 Enda Delaney, *The Irish in Postwar Britain* (Oxford, 2007), p. 90.

11 Letter to Thomas MacGreevy, 4 August 1932; quoted Cronin, *Samuel Beckett*, p. 179.

12 According to his brother, Joyce 'never liked' London. See Stanislaus Joyce, *My Brother's Keeper*, ed. Richard Ellmann, pref. T. S. Eliot (London, 1958), p. 197.

13 See Knowlson, *Damned to Fame*, p. 186, from which some of the other detail in this and the following paragraph also derives.

14 This, to judge from what he said of 'distress . . . screaming at [one] *even*

in the taxis of London'. See Tom F. Driver, 'Beckett by the Madeleine'
[interview], Columbia University Forum IV (Summer, 1961); repr.
Samuel Beckett: The Critical Heritage, ed. Lawrence Graver and
Raymond Federman (London, 1979), pp. 217–23 (p. 221), italics mine.
For 'Muttonfatville', see Knowlson, *Damned to Fame*, p. 512.

15 See Cronin, *Samuel Beckett*, p. 174.
16 According to Knowlson. See *Damned to Fame*, p. 186.
17 Delaney, *The Irish in Postwar Britain*, p. 10.
18 Knowlson, *Damned to Fame*, p. 202.
19 There is actually rather little in *Murphy* that very clearly suggests
   that the character might hail from a Protestant background. A 'Dutch
   uncle' (*MU*, p. 150) is not much to go on. The crucial factors are cultural,
   and Murphy shares them with Neary: Trinity College, Berkeley,
   a supercilious distaste for Gaelicism, and a stake in the (Protestant-
   dominated) Revivalist interest in the arcane and occult. Murphy's
   references to Blake have a flavour more Yeatsian than Joycean.
   Knowlson has amply shown how far and in what respects Murphy
   resembles Beckett. He also documents the connection between Neary
   and Trinity Professor H. S. Macran. See *Damned to Fame*, pp. 204–12.
20 Delaney, *The Irish in Postwar Britain*, p. 72.
21 James Klugmann, 'Introduction: The Crisis of the Thirties: A View
   from the Left', in Jon Clark, Margot Heinemann, David Margolies and
   Carole Snee, *Culture and Crisis in Britain in the Thirties* (London, 1979),
   pp. 13–36 (p. 29).
22 See Lois Gordon, *The World of Samuel Beckett 1906–1946* (New Haven
   and London, 1996), pp. 97–9.
23 *Pace* Gordon. See ibid., chap. 5 (pp. 92–125).
24 Klugmann, 'Introduction', p. 16.
25 Alice Prochaska, *London in the Thirties* (London, 1973), p. 5.
26 See J. B. Priestley, *English Journey: Being a Rambling but Truthful Account
   of What One Man Saw and Heard and Felt and Thought During a Journey
   Through England During the Autumn of the Year 1933* (London, 1934),
   pp. 248–9.
27 Liam Greenslade, 'White Skin, White Masks: Psychological Distress
   Among the Irish in Britain', in *The Irish World Wide: History, Heritage,
   Identity*, vol. II: *The Irish in the New Communities*, ed. P. O. Sullivan
   (Leicester and London, 1992), pp. 201–25 (p. 215).

28 See Elizabeth Malcolm, '"A Most Miserable Looking Object": The Irish in English Asylums 1851–1901: Migration, Poverty and Prejudice', in *Irish and Polish Migration in Comparative Perspective*, ed. John Belchem and Klaus Tenfelde (Essen, 2003), pp. 121–32 (p. 130).

29 See Ronan Fanning, *Independent Ireland* (Dublin, 1983), p. 143.

30 Maurice Moynihan, ed., *Speeches and Statements by Eamon de Valera 1917–73* (Dublin, 1980), p. 155.

31 Quoted Bernard G. Krimm, *W. B. Yeats and the Emergence of the Irish Free State* (Troy, NY, 1981), p. 230.

4 Melancholia *im dritten Reich*: Germany, 1936–7

1 As Mark Nixon asserts. See 'Becketts *German Diaries* der Deutschlandreise 1936–37: Eine Einführung zur Chronik' and 'Chronik der Deutschlandsreise Becketts 1936–37', in *Der Unbekannte Beckett: Samuel Beckett und die Deutsche Kultur*, ed. Marion Dieckmann-Fries and Therese Seidel (Frankfurt am Main, 2005), pp. 20–62 (p. 23).

2 See, among others, the entry for 24.10.36. Hitler is usually 'A.H.' from the start of the diaries. As Quadflieg points out, the *Hitlergruss* is often 'H.H.' See Roswitha Quadflieg, *Beckett Was Here: Hamburg im Tagebuch Samuel Becketts von 1936* (Hamburg, 2006), p. 47.

3 *Pace* Deirdre Bair. See *Samuel Beckett: A Biography* (London, 1990), pp. 259–60.

4 See Nixon, 'Becketts *German Diaries* der Deutschlandreise 1936–37' and 'Chronik der Deutschlandsreise Becketts 1936–37', pp. 24–5. But he adds that 'the tense atmosphere in the country is also perceptible on the edges of the Diaries', p. 24.

5 Though Nixon admirably demonstrates how and how far Beckett's experience of Germany contributed to his artistic development. See '"Writing": Die Bedeutung der Deutschlandreise 1936–37 für Becketts Schriftstellerische Entwicklung', in *Obergeschoss Still Closed – Samuel Beckett in Berlin*, ed. Lutz Dittrich, Carola Veit and Ernest Wichner, Texte aus dem Literaturhaus Berlin, Band 16 (Berlin, 2006), pp. 103–22.

6 As Bair again supposes. See *Samuel Beckett*, p. 260.

7 Hitler can be heard building to his hysterical climax at http://nsl-archiv.com/Tontraeger/Reden/Bis–1945/heil.php. The

Winterhilfswerk was collected for the relief of 'common [German] need' on the streets and at the doors of houses, by deductions from wages and salaries, and so on. See Quadflieg, *Beckett Was Here*, p. 29.

8 *GD*, 18.1.37; quoted Nixon, '"Writing"', p. 117.

9 Quadflieg, *Beckett Was Here*, p. 153.

10 Ibid., p. 83.

11 George Orwell, review of Johann Wöller, *Zest for Life*, *Time and Tide*, 17 October 1936; repr. *The Collected Essays, Journalism and Letters*, vol. I, *An Age Like This 1929–40*, ed. Sonia Orwell and Ian Angus (Boston, MA, 2004), pp. 234–5 (p. 234).

12 See also Quadflieg, *Beckett Was Here*, pp. 153, 155.

13 Nixon, '"Writing"', p. 112.

14 See her 'Beckett et la passion mélancolique: Une lecture de *Comment c'est*', in *L'Affect dans l'œuvre Beckettienne, Samuel Beckett Today/ Aujourd'hui*, ed. Matthijs Engelberts, Sjef Houppermans, Yann Mével and Michèle Touret, X (2000), pp. 39–52.

15 Quadflieg, *Beckett Was Here*, p. 66.

16 *GD*, 15.1.37; quoted Nixon, '"Writing"', p. 115.

17 See Quadflieg, *Beckett Was Here*, p. 81: 'for the Irishman, at some point, there had to be an end to "Gleichgeschaltetheit" [being forced into line]'.

18 The first in a letter to his friend A. J. Leventhal of 7 May 1934, the second in the *Whoroscope* notebook. Quoted Mark Nixon, 'Gospel und Verbot: Beckett und Nazi Deutschland', in *Das Raubauge in der Stadt: Beckett Liest Hamburg*, ed. Michaela Giesing, Gaby Hartel and Carola Veit (Göttingen, 2007), pp. 79–88 (p. 81).

19 A navy training ship used to get round the post-Versailles military restrictions.

20 But according to Quadflieg, Asher was the one person in Hamburg whom Beckett got wrong: her father was in fact of Jewish stock. Fear of repression had driven her sister and brother to flee Germany early in 1936. Her work for the Akademische Auslandstelle inclined her to adopt a conformist facade. See *Beckett Was Here*, pp. 58–60, 70. I am grateful to Mark Nixon for drawing this to my attention. It is worth noting, however, that Asher consistently supported apartheid in South Africa after the war. See *Beckett Was Here*, p. 136.

21 Notably in Prora, the vast, deserted, derelict *Kraft durch Freude* leisure

complex on Rügen.

22 Joan L. Clinefelter, *Artists for the Reich: Culture and Race from Weimar to Nazi Germany* (Oxford, 2005), p. 88.

23 David Addyman, 'Beckett and Place: The Lie of the Land', PhD thesis, University of London, 2008.

24 This is Quadflieg's view. She reads the Hamburg lists intelligently, as symptomatic of Beckett's condition of the time. See *Beckett Was Here*, p. 28. But her understanding of that condition is rooted in a mundane psychologism very similar to Knowlson's: astray in a strange city and much pressed by new sensations, Beckett needed handrails to guide him.

25 He had already used the word in *Dream of Fair to Middling Women*. See for instance *DFMW*, pp. 19, 36.

26 See Nixon, 'Gospel und Verbot', p. 81.

27 Pierre Ayçoberry, *The Social History of the Third Reich 1933–1945*, trans. Janet Lloyd (New York, 1999), p. 140.

28 *GD*, 18.10.36; quoted James Knowlson, *Damned to Fame: The Life of Samuel Beckett* (London, 1996), p. 233.

29 See for instance Adelheid von Saldern, *The Challenge of Modernity: German Social and Cultural Studies, 1890–1960*, trans. Bruce Little (Ann Arbor, MI, 2002), esp. pp. 317–18; and Lilian Karina, Marion Kant and Jonathan Steinberg, *Hitler's Dancers: German Modern Dance and the Third Reich*, trans. Jonathan Steinberg (Oxford and New York, 2003), pp. 81–2.

30 As Nixon exactly states. See 'Becketts *German Diaries* der Deutschlandreise 1936–37', p. 26.

31 See Quadflieg, *Beckett Was Here*, pp. 192–3.

32 See ibid., pp. 71–4. The quotations from the *Diaries* are at pp. 70, 116.

33 Quoted Knowlson, *Damned to Fame*, p. 261.

34 *GD*, 15.1.37; quoted Nixon, '"Writing"', p. 115.

35 Marjorie Perloff, in '"In Love with Hiding": Samuel Beckett's War', *Iowa Review*, xxxv/2 (2005), p. 93. She is thinking of the reference in the story to Agrippa d'Aubigné and his lament for the 'chesnes superbes' destroyed in battle. See *CSP*, p. 62.

36 In a letter of 9 October 1936. Quoted Nixon, 'Gospel und Verbot', p. 82.

37 *GD*, 15.11.36; quoted Knowlson, *Damned to Fame*, p. 237.

38 This is not to forget that *ez ozel*, 'the goat that escapes' or 'escape-goat', was actually a misreading of the Hebrew *Azazel* in Leviticus, one

perpetrated by the translators of the King James Bible.

39 I derive much of my account of the *pharmakos* from Todd M. Compton, *Victim of the Muses: Scapegoat, Warrior and Hero in Greco-Roman and Indo-European Myth and History* (Cambridge, MA, and London, 2006). For a list of the features of the *pharmakos*, see pp. 14–16.

40 Quoted in ibid., p. 5.

41 See Girard, *Violence and the Sacred*, trans. Patrick Gregory (Baltimore, MD, 1977); and *The Scapegoat*, trans. Yvonne Freccero (Baltimore, MD, 1986). Walter Burkert also argues that the Greek scapegoat appears in times of the imminence of war. See his *Structure and History in Greek Mythology* (Berkeley, CA, 1979).

42 For the Irish blame-poet, see Compton, *Victim of the Muses*, chap. 7, 'Kissing the Leper: The Excluded Poet in Irish Myth', pp. 193–217.

5 *Élimination des déchets*: The War, Resistance, Vichy France, 1939–44

1 Letter to Arland Ussher, 15 June 1937; quoted Deirdre Bair, *Samuel Beckett: A Biography* (London, 1990), p. 274.

2 See James Knowlson, *Damned to Fame: The Life of Samuel Beckett* (London, 1996), p. 266.

3 Letter to Thomas MacGreevy, 21 September 1937; quoted Bair, *Samuel Beckett*, p. 276.

4 Letter to Thomas MacGreevy, 23 August 1937; quoted Knowlson, *Damned to Fame*, p. 265.

5 Letter to Thomas MacGreevy, 28 September 1937; quoted Anthony Cronin, *Samuel Beckett: The Last Modernist* (London, 1996), p. 262.

6 Cronin, *Samuel Beckett*, pp. 262–3.

7 *Irish Times*, 24 November 1937; quoted Bair, *Samuel Beckett*, p. 284.

8 As Knowlson says, *Damned to Fame*, p. 295.

9 Letter to Thomas MacGreevy, 18 April 1939; quoted Knowlson, *Damned to Fame*, p. 297.

10 Lois Gordon is a conspicuous exception. But though she introduces Paxton's work with reference to Beckett, at the time she was writing, it was very much harder to grasp its full context, or its significance for

understanding Beckett and his career. See however Lois Gordon, *The World of Samuel Beckett 1906–1946* (New Haven and London, 1996), pp. 145–62.

11 For the term and concept and a commentary on them, see e.g. Jean-Pierre Azéma, 'The Paxtonian Revolution', in *France at War: Vichy and the Historians*, trans. David Lake, ed. Sarah Fishman, Laura Lee Downs, Ioannis Sinanoglou, Leonard V. Smith and Robert Zaretsky (Oxford, 2000), pp. 13–20.

12 Quoted *New York Times*, 17 July 1995.

13 Sarah Fishman and Leonard V. Smith, 'Introduction', in *France at War*, ed. Fishman et al., pp. 1–8 (p. 2).

14 See Henry Rousso, *The Vichy Syndrome: History and Memory in France Since 1944* (Cambridge, MA, and London, 1991), p. 58.

15 Ibid., esp. pp. 7–8.

16 Jean-Marie Guillon, 'La Résistance au village', in *La Résistance et les Français: Enjeux stratégiques et environnement*, ed. Jacqueline Sainclivier and Christian Bougeard (Rennes, 1995), pp. 233–43 (p. 235). See H. R. Kedward, 'Rural France and Resistance', in *France at War*, ed. Fishman et al., pp. 125–43, for an account of the 'radical complications' in question.

17 See for example Stanley Hoffman, 'Vichy Studies in France: Before and After Paxton', in *France at War*, ed. Fishman et al., pp. 49–60.

18 See Eric Conan and Henry Rousso, *Vichy: Un passé qui ne passe pas* (Paris, 1994). Their title of course translates Nolte's German.

19 Knowlson, *Damned to Fame*, p. 299.

20 See Conan and Rousso, *Vichy*, p. 171; and Jean-Pierre Azéma, 'Des résistances à la Résistance', in *La France des années noires*, vol. 2, *De l'occupation à la Libération*, ed. Jean-Pierre Azéma and François Bédarida (Paris, 1993), pp. 241–70 (p. 242).

21 Quoted H. R. Kedward, *Resistance in Vichy France* (Oxford, 1978), pp. 76–7.

22 See Dominique Veillon, *Vivre et survivre en France 1939–47* (Paris, 1995), p. 55. Hugh Kenner first suggested that the theme of waiting might be historical in origin. See *A Reader's Guide to Samuel Beckett* (Syracuse, NY, 1996), p. 30. Perloff fleshes out his brief argument. See Marjorie Perloff, '"In Love with Hiding": Samuel Beckett's War', *Iowa Review*, XXXV/2 (2005), esp. pp. 84–5. The historians allow us to add substance and precision to both.

23 See Veillon, *Vivre*, p. 254.

24 The word itself, however, appears to have entered the language during the First World War.

25 Robert Paxton, *Vichy France: Old Guard and the New Order 1940–1944*, revd edn (New York, 2001), p. 290.

26 Ibid., p. 293.

27 Ibid., p. 295.

28 For an example of this, see Roderick Kedward, 'The Maquis and the Culture of the Outlaw (with Particular Reference to the Cévennes)', in *Vichy France and the Resistance: Culture and Ideology*, ed. Roderick Kedward and Roger Austin (London, 1985), pp. 232–51 (p. 246).

29 See John F. Sweets, *Choices in Vichy France: The French Under Nazi Occupation* (Oxford, 1994), pp. 42–54.

30 Ibid., p. 60.

31 See W. D. Halls, *The Youth of Vichy France* (Oxford, 1981), p. 48.

32 See André Missenard's *Vers un homme meilleur . . . par la science expérimentale de l'homme* (Paris and Strasbourg, 1967). Though not published until 1967 – a date which rather stops one in one's tracks – this book was a major statement of the established principles of the Fondation. Missenard was one of its co-founders.

33 This never became public policy under Vichy.

34 Alexis Carrel, *L'Homme, cet inconnu* (Paris, 1935), p. 388.

35 Carrel's addition to Gustav Klipper, letter to Carrel, 16 December 1935; in the Alexis Carrel papers, Georgetown University Library, Box 70; quoted in Andrés Horacio Reggiani's highly instructive essay 'Alexis Carrel, The Unknown: Eugenics and Population Research Under Vichy', *French Historical Studies* xxv (2002), pp. 331–56 (p. 349). See also his monograph *God's Eugenicist: Alexis Carrel and the Sociobiography of Decline*, with a foreword by Herman Lebovics (Oxford and New York, 2006).

36 See Giorgio Agamben, *Homo Sacer: Sovereign Power and Bare Life*, trans. Daniel Heller-Roazen (Stanford, CA, 1998).

37 Unsourced quotation. See Jean-Pierre Rioux, 'Ambivalences en rouge et bleu: Les pratiques culturelles des Français pendant les années noires', in *La vie culturelle sous Vichy*, ed. Jean-Pierre Rioux (Brussels, 1990), pp. 41–60 (p. 45).

38 Dominique Veillon, 'The Resistance and Vichy', in *France at War*, ed.

Fishman et al., pp. 161–77 (p. 162).

39 Jean-Pierre Rioux, 'Everyday Culture in Occupied France', in *France at War*, ed. Fishman et al., pp. 221–9 (p. 223).

40 See Perloff, '"In Love with Hiding"', pp. 88–100. Perloff's claim is that they are chiefly concerned with and reflect a wartime life 'of hiding and attempted escape', p. 88.

41 See for instance Veillon, *Vivre*, p. 188.

42 See Sweets, *Choices in Vichy France*, pp. 103–4; and Veillon, *Vivre*, pp. 317, 321. 'Nourritures terrestres' is the title of the fourth chapter of her book, pp. 101–32. Cf. Paxton, *Vichy France*, p. 238: during the war, 'France was eventually the worst nourished of the Western occupied nations.'

6 *Indignités*: Liberation, the Purge, de Gaulle, 1944–9

1 Knowlson suggests Beckett returned in early 1945 but informs us that this has been disputed, James Knowlson, *Damned to Fame: The Life of Samuel Beckett* (London, 1996), pp. 340, 769, n.1. Cronin suggests November 1944 and cites a telegram from Beckett announcing his arrival, Anthony Cronin, *Samuel Beckett: The Last Modernist* (London, 1996), p. 340.

2 Interview with Lawrence Harvey, undated; quoted Knowlson, *Damned to Fame*, p. 340.

3 Quoted Cronin, *Samuel Beckett*, p. 340.

4 Letter to Freda Young; quoted Cronin, *Samuel Beckett*, p. 343.

5 Clair Wills brings out the originality of Beckett's position in an Irish context. See *That Neutral Island: A History of Ireland During the Second World War* (London, 2007), pp. 413–14.

6 Quoted Ronan Fanning, *Independent Ireland* (Dublin, 1983), p. 128.

7 Letter to Tom MacGreevy, 19 August, 1945; quoted Knowlson, *Damned to Fame*, p. 345.

8 Gordon briefly discusses the Purge, but in the context of a brusque declaration that it was 'a psychological and moral necessity'. This premise seems to me to be not so much necessarily wrong as unhelpful with reference to Beckett and the *Trilogy*. But see Lois Gordon, *The World of Samuel Beckett 1906–1946* (New Haven and London, 1996), pp. 187–9.

9 *Combat*, 2 September 1944.

10 Robert Aron, *Histoire de l'épuration*, 4 vols (Paris, 1976), vol. I, p. 241.

11 René de Chambrun, *Pierre Laval devant l'histoire* (Paris, 1983), p. 275.

12 See Hubert Cole, *Laval: A Biography* (London, 1963), p. 282.

13 Herbert R. Lottman, *The Purge* (New York, 1986), p. 77.

14 Accessed at www.charles-de-gaulle.org/article.php3?id_article=514.

15 Robert Gildea, *Marianne in Chains: In Search of the German Occupation 1940–1945* (London, 2002), p. 378.

16 Marguerite Duras, *La douleur* (Paris, 1985), p. 41.

17 Henry Rousso, *The Vichy Syndrome: History and Memory in France Since 1944* (Cambridge, MA, and London, 1991), p. 17.

18 See Diane Rubenstein, *What's Left? The École Normale and the Right* (Madison, WI, 1990), p. 140.

19 See Lottman, *The Purge*, p. 76.

20 Ibid., p. 48.

21 Quoted Cronin, *Samuel Beckett*, p. 341.

22 See letter to MacGreevy, 19 August, 1945; quoted Knowlson, *Damned to Fame*, p. 346.

23 Letter to MacGreevy, 4 January, 1948; quoted Knowlson, *Damned to Fame*, p. 354.

24 To various people at various times; quoted Cronin, *Samuel Beckett*, p. 364.

25 Letters to Alan Schneider; quoted Cronin, *Samuel Beckett*, pp. 459, 462.

26 See Knowlson, 'Samuel Beckett: The Intricate Web of Life and Work', *Journal of Beckett Studies*, XVI/1–2 (Fall 2006/Summer 2007), pp. 17–29 (p. 23); and *GD*, 31.10.36; quoted Roswitha Quadflieg, *Beckett Was Here: Hamburg im Tagebuch Samuel Becketts von 1936* (Hamburg, 2006), p. 90.

27 Cf. Clair Wills's account on Beckett's writings in the late 1940s, *That Neutral Island*, p. 414.

28 See Knowlson, *Damned to Fame*, p. 453.

29 I am grateful to Lorna Mellon for this point. The 'difference' is that, in the twentieth-century version, the lower of the two horizontals is longer than the upper, and both are closer to the top of the vertical than the bottom.

30 Quoted Jean-Louis Crémieux-Brilhac, *Les voix de la liberté: Ici Londres (1940–44)*, 5 vols (Paris, 1975), vol. IV, p. 245.

31 See Sir James Frazer, *The Golden Bough: A Study in Magic and Religion*, 3rd edn (Basingstoke, 2002), Part III, *The Dying God*, especially chap. 6, 'Sacrifice of the King's Son', pp. 160–95; and Part VI, *The Scapegoat*, especially pp. 198–223; VI, p. 72.

32 Ibid., VI, p. 212.

33 Ibid., VI, p. 222.

34 Ibid., VI, p. 72.

35 *La résistance savoyarde*, 1 September 1945; quoted Megan Koreman, *The Expectation of Justice* (Durham, NC, 1999), p. 93.

36 Petronius, *The Satyricon*, trans. with intro. and notes by J. P. Sullivan (Harmondsworth, 1987), pp. 96–101.

7 Make Sense Who May: A World at Cold War, 1950–85

1 *Daily Mail*, 4 August 1955; quoted James Knowlson, *Damned to Fame: The Life of Samuel Beckett* (London, 1996), p. 415.

2 Letter to Thomas MacGreevy, 7 August 1985; quoted Anthony Cronin, *Samuel Beckett: The Last Modernist* (London, 1996), p. 448.

3 Patsy Southgate, 'Rosset Remembers Beckett', *Summer Book Supplement to the East Hampton Star and the Sag Harbor Herald*, 24 May 1990; quoted Knowlson, *Damned to Fame*, p. 525.

4 Cluchey was sentenced to life, but the sentence was subsequently commuted. See Knowlson, *Damned to Fame*, p. 611.

5 *GD*, 6.11.36; quoted Roswitha Quadflieg, *Beckett Was Here: Hamburg im Tagebuch Samuel Becketts von 1936* (Hamburg, 2006), p. 107.

6 Letter to Tom MacGreevy, 11 August 1955; quoted Knowlson, *Damned to Fame*, p. 390.

7 Letter to Henry Wenning, 31 July 1963; quoted Knowlson, *Damned to Fame*, p. 507.

8 Unsourced quotation, Steve Phillips, *The Cold War* (Oxford, 2001), p. 163.

9 '1954: Portrait of the Year', *Times*, 1 January 1955, p. 1.

10 Andrew J. Dunan, *America in the Fifties*, with a foreword by John Robert Greene (New York, 2006), p. 134.

11 See http://en.wikipedia.org/wiki/Massive_retaliation.

12 *Life*, 16 January 1956. The term 'brinkmanship' itself was originally

coined by Adlai Stevenson.

13 Charles A. Carpenter, *Dramatists and the Bomb: American and British Playwrights Confront the Nuclear Age 1945–1964*, Contributions in Drama and Theatre Studies, no. 9 (Westport, CT, 1999), p. 55.

14 Dougald McMillan and Martha Fehsenfeld, *Beckett in the Theatre: The Author as Practical Playwright and Director* (London and New York, 1988), p. 174.

15 Frances Stonor Sanders, *Who Paid the Piper? The CIA and the Cultural Cold War* (London, 1999). See also Hugh Wilford, 'Calling the Tune? The CIA, the British Left and the Cold War, 1945–1960', in *The Cultural Cold War in Western Europe 1945–1960*, ed. Giles Scott-Smith and Hans Krabberdam (London and Portland, 2003), pp. 41–50.

16 McMillan and Fehsenfeld, *Beckett in the Theatre*, p. 204.

17 *Theatrical Notebooks*, general ed. James Knowlson, vol. II, *Endgame*, ed. with intro. and notes by S. E. Gontarski (London, 1992), p. 43.

18 Unsourced quotation, John Calder, *Samuel Beckett: A Personal Memoir*, accessible at www.naxosaudiobooks.com/PAGES/beckettmemories.htm.

19 This, in different forms, was a longstanding Beckettian theme. For an account of *Murphy* which takes it into consideration, see Andrew Gibson, *Beckett and Badiou: The Pathos of Intermittency* (Oxford, 2006), pp. 143–55.

20 For Adorno's essay 'Towards an Understanding of *Endgame*', see *Twentieth Century Interpretations of 'Endgame'*, ed. Ruth Gale Chevigny (Englewood Cliffs, NJ, 1969), pp. 82–114.

21 See for instance William A. Williams, *The Tragedy of American Diplomacy* (Cleveland and New York, 1959); Gar Alperowitz, *Cold War Essays*, intro. Christopher Lasch (New York, 1970); Joyce and Gabriel Kolko, *The Limits of Power: The World and US Foreign Policy 1945–1954* (New York, 1972); and William O. McCagg, *Stalin Embattled 1943–48* (Detroit, MI, 1978). Revisionism later gave way to what recent historians frequently claim is the greater detachment of a (rather un-Beckettian) 'post-revisionism'.

22 See Knowlson, *Damned to Fame*, p. 680.

23 In his notebook for the Schiller-Theater production of *Godot* in 1975. See *Theatrical Notebooks*, vol. IV: *The Shorter Plays*, ed. with an intro. and notes by S. E. Gontarski (London and New York, 1999), p. 93.

8 Where He Happened To Be: Capital *Triumphans*, 1985–9

1 See Francis Fukuyama, 'The End of History?', *The National Interest*, xvi
   (Summer 1989), pp. 3–18; and *The End of History and the Last Man*
   (New York, 1992).

2 See Anthony Cronin, *Samuel Beckett: The Last Modernist* (London,
   1996), p. 591.

3 Cf. his dismissal of 'easy solutions' elsewhere. See for example Dr Hans
   Joachim Schaefer, 'Memories of a Meeting with Beckett and his Wife',
   to Dr Gottfried Büttner, 16 November 1989, quoted James Knowlson,
   Damned to Fame: The Life of Samuel Beckett (London, 1996), p. 477.

4 J. M. Coetzee, *Inner Workings: Literary Essays 2000–2005*, intro. Derek
   Attridge (London, 2008), p. 289.

5 Letter to Barney Rosset, 23 November 1958; quoted Cronin, *Samuel
   Beckett*, p. 476.

6 Card to Lawrence Harvey, 30 April 1962; quoted Knowlson, *Damned to
   Fame*, p. 498.

7 Letter to Thomas MacGreevy, 28 August 1934; quoted Knowlson,
   Damned to Fame, p. 175.

8 Ronald Hayman, *Writing Against: A Biography of Sartre* (London, 1986),
   pp. 58, 76–7, 123.

9 Letter to A. J. Leventhal, 11 December 1957; quoted Knowlson, *Damned
   to Fame*, p. 442.

10 Cronin, *Samuel Beckett*, p. 510.

11 Knowlson, *Damned to Fame*, p. 388.

12 See Cronin, *Samuel Beckett*, p. 591.

13 Knowlson, *Damned to Fame*, p. 408. Knowlson is quoting from his
   interview with Jamet, 3 July 1991.

14 In interview with Knowlson, 27 October 1989; see *Damned to Fame*, p. 352;
   and Ludovic Janvier, *Samuel Beckett par lui-même* (Paris, 1969), (p. 18).

15 Steven Connor, 'Absolute Rubbish: Cultural Economies of Loss in
   Freud, Bataille and Beckett', in *Theory and Cultural Value* (Oxford,
   1992), pp. 57–101 (p. 80).

16 George Perec, *Life: A User's Manual*, trans. David Bellos (London,
   1987), p. 61.

17 *GD* 5.11.36; quoted Mark Nixon, '"Writing": Die Bedeutung der
   Deutschlandreise 1936–37 für Becketts Schriftstellerische Entwicklung',

in *Obergeschoss Still Closed – Samuel Beckett in Berlin*, ed. Lutz Dittrich, Carola Veit and Ernest Wichner, Texte aus dem Literaturhaus Berlin, Band 16 (Berlin, 2006), pp. 103–22 (p. 108).

18 Simon Critchley, *Very Little . . . Almost Nothing: Death, Philosophy, Literature* (London, 1997), p. 22.

19 Theodor Adorno, *Negative Dialectics*, trans. E. B. Ashton (New York, 1973), p. 381; quoted *Very Little . . . Almost Nothing*, p. 24.

20 Ibid., p. 24.

Afterword: To Begin Yet Again

1 The term is Steven Connor's. See 'Slow Going', *Yearbook of English Studies*, xxx (2000), pp. 153–65.

2 James Joyce, *Ulysses*, ed. Hans Walter Gabler, with Wolfhard Steppe and Claus Melchior, afterword by Michael Groden (New York and London, 1984, 1986), 9.550–51.

3 Letter to Barney Rosset, 17 December 1957; quoted James Knowlson, *Damned to Fame: The Life of Samuel Beckett* (London, 1996), p. 431.

4 In Lawrence Harvey, notes on conversations with Beckett; quoted Knowlson, *Damned to Fame*, p. 492.

5 *What is to be Done?* I owe the point to Laura Salisbury, 'Beckett's Laughing Matters: Comedy, Time and Form in the Prose and Drama', PhD thesis, University of London, 2003, p. 43. Of course, for decades, the Marxist tradition dismissed melancholia out of hand as a bourgeois failure to coincide with the direction of history. History duly took its revenge.

6 In interview with Anthony Cronin; quoted *Samuel Beckett: The Last Modernist* (London, 1996), p. 518, where the word is 'hyperaesthesia'.

7 See Marjorie Perloff, '"In Love with Hiding": Samuel Beckett's War', *Iowa Review*, xxxv/2 (2005), p. 77–8; Maurice Nadeau, review of *Molloy, Combat*, 12 April 1951, in *Samuel Beckett: The Critical Heritage*, ed. Lawrence Graver and Raymond Federman (London, 1979), pp. 50–54; Georges Bataille, review of *Molloy*, in *Critique*, 15 May 1951, in *Samuel Beckett*, ed. Graver and Federman, pp. 55–64; Jean-Jacques Mayoux, 'Samuel Beckett and Universal Parody', in *Samuel Beckett: A Collection of Critical Essays*, ed. Martin Esslin (Englewood Cliffs, NJ,

1965), pp. 77–91; and Maurice Blanchot, *Le livre à venir* (Paris, 1959), pp. 308–15. For Casanova's arresting argument regarding Blanchot's Beckett, see *Samuel Beckett: Anatomy of a Literary Revolution*, trans. Gregory Elliot, intro. Terry Eagleton (London, 2006), 'Preface', pp. 10–13.

8 This is not to make an issue (again) of Bataille's flirtations with fascism or Blanchot's contributions to anti-Semitic journals. Neither are important here. My point is simply that both undeniably had reason to feel a certain discomfort after 1945, and that this should not be forgotten in assessments of the anti-historical drive in their readings of Beckett.

9 See Tom F. Driver, 'Beckett by the Madeleine' [interview], Columbia University Forum IV (Summer, 1961); repr. *Samuel Beckett*, ed. Graver and Federman, pp. 217–23 (p. 220).

10 Leo Bersani and Ulysse Dutoit, *Arts of Impoverishment; Beckett, Rothko, Resnais* (Cambridge, MA, and London, 1993), p. 19.

11 According to Martin Esslin. See Knowlson, *Damned to Fame*, p. 605 and p. 817, n.175.

12 Dr Hans Joachim Schaefer, 'Memories of a Meeting with Beckett and his Wife', to Dr Gottfried Büttner, 16 November 1989, quoted Knowlson, *Damned to Fame*, p. 477; and Charles Juliet, *Rencontres avec Samuel Beckett* (Montpelier, 1986), p. 28.

13 Vivian Mercier, *Beckett/Beckett* (New York, 1979), p. 121; quoted Cronin, *Samuel Beckett*, p. 467.

14 Knowlson, *Damned to Fame*, pp. 371–2. Knowlson is quoting an undated interview Beckett gave to Lawrence Harvey. The words 'depend' and 'record' are italicized in Knowlson's later version of the quotation, but it is not clear that this is the more accurate version. See James Knowlson, 'Samuel Beckett: The Intricate Web of Life and Work', *Journal of Beckett Studies*, XVI/1–2 (Fall 2006/Summer 2007), p. 17.

15 James Joyce, 'The Holy Office', in *Critical Writings*, ed. Ellsworth Mason and Richard Ellmann (London, 1959), pp. 149, 151.

16 Letter to Alan Schneider, 11 January 1956; quoted Knowlson, *Damned to Fame*, p. 420.

17 Letter to Pamela Mitchell, 23 February 1955; quoted Knowlson, *Damned to Fame*, p. 405.

18 Letter to Beckett, 17 April 1983; quoted Knowlson, *Damned to Fame*, p. 681.

19 *GD*, 14.2.37; quoted Knowlson, *Damned to Fame*, p. 254. Friedrich's 'flattened' romanticism can partly be thought through in terms of event and remainder with reference to his political experience and leanings in the second decade of the nineteenth century. See Werner Hoffman, *Caspar David Friedrich* (London, 2007), pp. 85–99.

Select Bibliography

Work

'Dante . . . Bruno. Vico . . . Joyce', in *Our Exagmination round His Factification for Incamination of Work in Progress* (Paris, 1929)

Proust (London, 1931)

More Pricks than Kicks [1934] (London, 1973)

Murphy [1938] (London, 1963)

Molloy (Paris, 1951)

Malone meurt (Paris, 1951)

L'Innommable (Paris, 1951)

Nouvelles et textes pour rien (Paris, 1951)

En attendant Godot: Pièce en deux actes, ed. Colin Duckworth, foreword Harold Hobson [1952] (Walton-on-Thames, 1985)

Watt [1953] (London, 1963)

Trilogy: Molloy, Malone Dies, The Unnamable [1959] (*Molloy* trans. the author in collaboration with Patrick Bowles, *Malone Dies* and *The Unnamable* trans. the author; London, 1994)

Comment c'est (Paris, 1961)

How It Is (London, 1964)

Assez (Paris, 1966)

Sans (Paris, 1969)

Mercier et Camier (Paris, 1970)

Têtes-Mortes (Paris, 1972)

Mercier and Camier (London, 1974)

Company (London, 1979)

Ill Seen Ill Said (London, 1981)

Mal vu mal dit (Paris, 1981)

Disjecta: Miscellaneous Writings and a Dramatic Fragment, ed. with a
    foreword Ruby Cohn (London, 1983)
Worstward Ho (London, 1983)
Collected Poems 1930–1978 (London, 1986)
Stirrings Still, illustrations by Louis Le Brocquy (London, 1988)
The Complete Dramatic Works (London, 1990)
Cap au pire, trans. Edith Fournier (Paris, 1991)
Dream of Fair to Middling Women (Dublin, 1992)
Theatrical Notebooks, general ed. James Knowlson, vol. II, *Endgame*, ed.
    with intro. and notes S. E. Gontarski (London, 1992)
Theatrical Notebooks, vol. III, *Krapp's Last Tape*, ed. with intro. and notes
    James Knowlson (London, 1992)
Theatrical Notebooks, vol. I, *Waiting for Godot*, ed. with intro. and notes
    Dougald MacMillan and James Knowlson (London, 1993)
The Complete Shorter Prose 1929–1989, ed. with intro. and notes
    S. E. Gontarski (New York, 1995)
Eleuthéria, trans. Michael Brodsky, with a foreword Martin Garbus and
    intro. S. E. Gontarski (New York, 1995)
Theatrical Notebooks, vol. IV: *The Shorter Plays*, ed. with intro. and notes
    S. E. Gontarski (London and New York, 1999) .

Biography

Bair, Deirdre, *Samuel Beckett: A Biography* (London, 1990)
Cronin, Anthony, *Samuel Beckett: The Last Modernist* (London, 1996)
Gordon, Lois, *The World of Samuel Beckett 1906–1946* (New Haven and
    London, 1996)
Knowlson, James, *Damned to Fame: The Life of Samuel Beckett* (London, 1996)
—, 'Samuel Beckett: The Intricate Web of Life and Work', *Journal of Beckett
    Studies*, XVI/1–2 (Fall 2006/Summer 2007), pp. 17–29
Nixon, Mark, 'Becketts *German Diaries* der Deutschlandreise 1936–37: Eine
    Einführung zur Chronik' and 'Chronik der Deutschlandsreise Becketts
    1936-37', in *Der Unbekannte Beckett: Samuel Beckett und die Deutsche
    Kultur*, ed. Marion Dieckmann-Fries and Therese Seidel (Frankfurt am
    Main, 2005), pp. 20–62
—, 'Gospel und Verbot: Beckett und Nazi Deutschland', in *Das Raubauge in*

der Stadt: Beckett Liest Hamburg, ed. Michaela Giesing, Gaby Hartel and
    Carola Veit (Göttingen, 2007), pp. 79–88
Quadflieg, Roswitha, *Beckett Was Here: Hamburg im Tagebuch Samuel Becketts*
    von 1936 (Hamburg, 2006)

Criticism

Abbott, H. Porter, *The Fiction of Samuel Beckett: Form and Effect* (Berkeley, CA,
    1973)
—, *Beckett Writing Beckett: The Author in the Autograph* (Ithaca and London,
    1996)
Acheson, James, *Samuel Beckett's Artistic Theory and Practice* (London, 1997)
—, and Kateryna Arthur, eds, *Beckett's Later Fiction and Drama*, with a
    foreword by Melvin J. Friedman (London, 1987)
Ackerley, C. J., *Demented Particulars: The Annotated 'Murphy', Journal of
    Beckett Studies*, VII/1–2 (Autumn 1997, Spring 1998)
Addyman, David, 'Beckett and Place: The Lie of the Land', PhD thesis,
    University of London, 2008
Admussen, Richard, *The Samuel Beckett Manuscripts* (Boston, MA, 1979)
Astier, Pierre, 'Beckett's *Ohio Impromptu*: A View from the Swans', *Modern
    Drama*, XXV/3 (1982), pp. 331–48
Badiou, Alain, *Samuel Beckett: L'Écriture du générique et l'amour* (Paris, 1989)
—, *Beckett: L'increvable désir* (Paris, 1995)
—, *On Beckett*, trans. and intro. Nina Power and Alberto Toscano, with a
    preface by Alain Badiou and a postface by Andrew Gibson (Manchester,
    2003)
Baker, Phil, *Beckett and the Mythology of Psychoanalysis* (London, 1997)
Barnard, C. G., *Samuel Beckett: A New Approach* (London, 1970)
Begam, Richard, *Samuel Beckett and the End of Modernity* (Stanford, CA, 1996)
Beja, Morris, S. E. Gontarski and Pierre Astier, eds, *Samuel Beckett:
    Humanistic Perspectives* (Columbus, OH, 1983)
Bernal, Olga, *Langage et fiction dans le roman de Beckett* (Paris, 1969)
Bersani, Leo and Ulysse Dutoit, *Arts of Impoverishment: Beckett, Rothko,
    Resnais* (Cambridge, MA, and London, 1993)
Brater, Enoch, ed., *Beckett at 80: Beckett in Context* (Oxford, 1986)
—, *Beyond Minimalism: Beckett's Late Style in the Theatre* (Oxford, 1987)

Brienza, Susan D., *Samuel Beckett's New Worlds: Style in Metafiction* (Norman and London, 1987)

Bryden, Mary, *Women in Samuel Beckett's Prose and Drama: Her Own Other* (London, 1993)

—, *Samuel Beckett and the Idea of God* (Basingstoke, 1998)

Buning, Marius and Lois Oppenheim, eds, *Beckett in the 1990s* (Amsterdam and Atlanta, 1993)

—, Matthijs Engelberts, Sjef Houppermans and Danièle de Ruyter-Tognotti, eds, *Three Dialogues Revisited*, Samuel Beckett Today/Aujourd'hui, XIII (2003)

Butler, Lance St. John, *Samuel Beckett and the Meaning of Being: A Study in Ontological Parable* (London, 1985)

Casanova, Pascale, *Samuel Beckett: Anatomy of a Literary Revolution*, trans. Gregory Elliot, intro. Terry Eagleton (London, 2006)

Caselli, Daniela, *Beckett's Dantes: Intertextuality in the Fiction and Criticism* (Manchester, 2006)

Clément, Bruno, *L'Œuvre sans qualités: Rhétorique de Samuel Beckett* (Paris, 1994)

Coe, Richard, *Beckett* (Edinburgh and London, 1964)

Cohn, Ruby, *Samuel Beckett: The Comic Gamut* (New Brunswick, NJ, 1962)

—, *Back to Beckett* (Princeton, NJ, 1973)

Connor, Steven, *Samuel Beckett: Repetition, Theory and Text* (Oxford, 1988)

—, ed., '*Waiting for Godot' and 'Endgame'* (London, 1992)

—, 'Absolute Rubbish: Cultural Economies of Loss in Freud, Bataille and Beckett', in *Theory and Cultural Value* (Oxford, 1992), pp. 57–101

—, 'Slow Going', *Yearbook of English Studies*, XXX (2000), pp. 153–65

Critchley, Simon, *Very Little . . . Almost Nothing: Death, Philosophy, Literature* (London, 1997)

Dearlove, Judith, *Accommodating the Chaos: Samuel Beckett's Nonrelational Art* (Durham, NC, 1982)

Driver, Tom F., 'Beckett by the Madeleine' [interview], Columbia University Forum IV (Summer, 1961); repr. *Samuel Beckett*, ed. Graver and Federman, pp. 217–23

Engelberts, Matthijs, Sjef Houppermans, Yann Mével and Michèle Touret, eds, *L'Affect dans l'œuvre Beckettienne*, Samuel Beckett Today/Aujourd'hui, X (2000)

Esslin, Martin, *The Theatre of the Absurd* (Harmondsworth, 1968)

Federman, Raymond, *Journey to Chaos: Samuel Beckett's Early Fiction* (Berkeley and Los Angeles, 1970)

Feldman, Matthew, *Beckett's Books: A Cultural History of Samuel Beckett's 'Interwar Notes'* (London, 2006)

—, and Mark Nixon, eds, *Beckett's Literary Legacies* (Cambridge, 2007)

Finney, Brian, *Since 'How It Is': A Study of Samuel Beckett's Later Fiction* (London, 1972)

Fournier, Edith, 'Samuel Beckett, mathématicien et poète', *Critique*, XLVI (1990), pp. 660–69

Gibson, Andrew, 'Les Économies de *Murphy*', in *L'Affect dans l'œuvre Beckettienne*, ed. Engelberts et al., pp. 85–96

—, '*Three Dialogues* and Beckett's Tragic Ethics', in *Three Dialogues Revisited, Samuel Beckett Today/Aujourd'hui*, Buning et al., pp. 43–54

—, *Beckett and Badiou: The Pathos of Intermittency* (Oxford, 2006)

Gontarski, S. E., *The Intent of Undoing in Samuel Beckett's Dramatic Texts* (Bloomington, IN, 1985)

Graver, Lawrence, and Raymond Federman, eds, *Samuel Beckett: The Critical Heritage* (London, Henley and Boston, MA, 1979)

Grossman, Evelyne, 'Beckett et la passion mélancolique: Une lecture de *Comment c'est*', in *L'Affect dans l'œuvre Beckettienne*, ed. Engelberts et al., pp. 39–52

Hansford, James, '*The Lost Ones*: The One and the Many', *Studies in Short Fiction*, XXVI/2 (Spring 1989), pp. 125–33

Harvey, Lawrence E., *Samuel Beckett: Poet and Critic* (Princeton, NJ, 1970)

Henning, Sylvie Debevec, *Beckett's Critical Complicity: Carnival, Contestation and Tradition* (Lexington, KT, 1988)

Hesla, David, *The Shape of Chaos: An Interpretation of the Art of Samuel Beckett* (Minneapolis, MN, 1971)

Hill, Leslie, *Beckett's Fiction: In Different Words* (Cambridge, 1990)

Hunkeler, Thomas, *Échos de l'ego dans l'œuvre de Samuel Beckett* (Paris, 1997)

Janvier, Ludovic, *Samuel Beckett par lui-même* (Paris, 1969)

Juliet, Charles, *Rencontres avec Samuel Beckett* (Montpelier, 1986)

—, *Conversations with Samuel Beckett and Bram van Velde*, trans. Janey Tucker (Leiden, 1995)

Kalb, Jonathan, *Beckett in Performance* (Cambridge, 1989)

Katz, Daniel, *Saying 'I' No More: Subjectivity and Consciousness in the Prose of Samuel Beckett* (Evanston, IL, 1999)

Kennedy, Sean, ed., *Beckett and Ireland* (Cambridge, forthcoming)

—, ed., *Samuel Beckett: History, Memory, Archive* (London, forthcoming)

Kenner, Hugh, *Samuel Beckett: A Critical Study* (London, 1968)

—, *A Reader's Guide to Samuel Beckett* (London, 1973)

Lane, Richard, ed., *Beckett and Philosophy* (Cambridge, MA, 2002)

Levy, Eric P., *Samuel Beckett and The Voice of Species* (Towota, NJ, 1980)

Libera, Antoni, '*The Lost Ones*: A Myth of Human History and Destiny',
    in *Samuel Beckett*, ed. Beja et al., pp. 145–56

Locatelli, Carla, *Unwording the Word: Samuel Beckett's Prose Works After the
    Nobel Prize* (Philadelphia, PA, 1990)

Maude, Ulrika, *Beckett, Technology and the Body* (Cambridge, 2009)

McMillan, Dougald, and Martha Fehsenfeld, *Beckett in the Theatre*
    (London, 1988)

McMullan, Anna, *Theatre on Trial: Samuel Beckett's Later Drama*
    (New York and London, 1993)

Mercier, Vivian, *Beckett/Beckett* (New York, 1979)

Moorjani, Angela, *Abysmal Games in the Novels of Samuel Beckett*
    (Chapel Hill, NC, 1982)

Morot-Sir, Edouard, H. Harper and Dougald McMillan, eds, *Samuel Beckett:
    The Art of Rhetoric* (Chapel Hill, NC, 1976)

Murphy, P.J., *Reconstructing Beckett: Language for Being in Samuel Beckett's
    Fiction* (Toronto, 1990)

Nixon, Mark, 'Writing "I": Samuel Beckett's *German Diaries*', *Journal of
    Beckett Studies*, XIII/2 (Spring 2004), pp. 10–23; reprinted in *Beckett the
    European*, ed. Dirk van Hulle (Tallahassee, FL, 2005), pp. 10–23

—, 'The *German Diaries* 1936–37: Beckett und die Moderne Deutsche
    Literatur', in *Der Unbekannte Beckett: Samuel Beckett und die Deutsche
    Kultur*, ed. Marion Dieckmann-Fries and Therese Seidel (Frankfurt am
    Main, 2005), pp. 138–54

—, '"Writing": Die Bedeutung der Deutschlandreise 1936–37 für Becketts
    Schriftstellerische Entwicklung', in: *Obergeschoss Still Closed – Samuel
    Beckett in Berlin*, ed. Lutz Dittrich, Carola Veit and Ernest Wichner,
    Texte aus dem Literaturhaus Berlin, Band 16 (Berlin, 2006), pp. 103–22

Oppenheim, Lois, *The Painted Word: Samuel Beckett's Dialogue with Art*
    (Ann Arbor, MI, 2000)

Perloff, Marjorie, '"In Love with Hiding": Samuel Beckett's War',
    Iowa Review, XXXV/2 (2005), pp. 76–103

Pilling, John, and James Knowlson, *Frescoes of the Skull: The Later Prose and Drama of Samuel Beckett* (London, 1979)

—, and Mary Bryden, eds, *The Ideal Core of the Onion: Reading Beckett Archives* (Reading, 1992)

—, ed., *The Cambridge Companion to Beckett* (Cambridge, 1994)

—, *Beckett Before Godot* (Cambridge, 1997)

Rabaté, Jean-Michel, *Beckett avant Beckett* (Paris, 1984)

Rabinovitz, Rubin, *The Development of Samuel Beckett's Fiction* (Urbana and Chicago, 1984)

—, 'The Self Contained: Beckett's Fiction in the 1960s', in *Beckett's Later Fiction and Drama*, ed. Acheson and Arthur, pp. 50–64

Ricks, Christopher, *Beckett's Dying Words* (Oxford, 1993)

Robinson, Michael, *The Long Sonata of the Dead* (London, 1969)

Rosen, Steven, *Beckett and the Pessimistic Tradition* (New Brunswick, NJ, 1976)

Salisbury, Laura, 'Beckett's Laughing Matters: Comedy, Time and Form in the Prose and Drama', PhD thesis, University of London, 2003

Scherzer, Dina, *Structure de la Trilogie de Beckett: Molloy, Malone meurt, L'Innommable* (The Hague, 1976)

Schwab, Gabriele, 'The Politics of Small Differences: Beckett's *The Unnamable*', in *Engagement and Indifference*, ed. Sussman and Devenney, pp. 42–57

Sussman, Henry, and Christopher Devenney, eds, *Engagement and Indifference: Beckett and the Political* (Albany, NY, 2001)

Tajiri, Yoshiki, *Samuel Beckett and the Prosthetic Body* (London, 2007)

Trezise, Thomas, *Into the Breach: Samuel Beckett and the Ends of Literature* (Princeton, NJ, 1990)

Uhlmann, Anthony, *Beckett and Poststructuralism* (Cambridge, 1999)

Ulin, Julieann, '"Buried! Who Would Have Buried Her?": Famine Ghost-Graves in Samuel Beckett's *Endgame*', in *Hungry Words: Images of Famine in the Irish Canon*, ed. George Cusack and Sarah Gross (Dublin, 2006), pp. 197–222

Watson, David, *Paradox and Desire in Samuel Beckett's Fiction* (London, 1990)

Weller, Shane, *A Taste for the Negative: Beckett and Nihilism* (London, 2005)

—, *Beckett, Literature and the Ethics of Alterity* (London, 2006)

Worth, Katharine, ed., *Beckett the Shape Changer* (London, 1975)

—, *Samuel Beckett's Theatre: Life Journeys* (Oxford, 1999)

Zurbrugg, Nicholas, *Beckett and Proust* (Gerrards Cross, 1988)

Acknowledgements

I am grateful to a number of different individuals who supplied me with useful information: David Addyman, Mary Daly, Anne Fogarty, Dan Katz, Sean Kennedy, Declan Kiberd and Laura Salisbury; and to others who read and commented on parts or the whole of the first draft: Joe Brooker, Ronan McDonald, Lenya Samanis and Yoshiki Tajiri. I owe a particular debt to Christian Egners and above all Mark Nixon for their assistance with Beckett's *German Diaries*. My thanks to Gina di Salvo for some of the information and quotations in chapter Seven. I am grateful as ever for the help of librarians in the British Library and the Bibliothèque Nationale in Paris and, in this instance, to librarians in Special Collections at the University of Reading. For a second time, Harry Gilonis, picture editor at Reaktion Books, was not only enthusiastic but indefatigable, and helped me in a number of different and important ways. Vivian Constantinopoulos, editor at Reaktion, was wise, patient, judicious and encouraging.

My major debt is to staff and students in the English Department at Northwestern University where I served as Carole and Gordon Segal Professor of Irish Literature for 2008. They talked, listened, made suggestions, restrained me from intellectual excesses. I am grateful above all to the students in my graduate seminar. Initially sceptical about the possibility of historicizing Beckett, they quickly became extraordinarily responsive to the idea, whilst pursuing it in their own distinctive ways. Parts of this book are theirs as well as mine. I acknowledge particular debts where appropriate. None of the above is responsible for any errors that may appear in my text.

Portions of the book were first presented as or in papers: 'Historical Spectres in Beckett's *Trilogie*', 'Spectres of Beckett/Spectral Beckett', inaugural conference of *Limit(e)-Beckett*, Université de Paris IV and VII, 2009; and

'Beckett and the Irish Diaspora: *Murphy* as Migrant Novel', Research Seminar, English Department, Northwestern University, 2008.

Photo Acknowledgements

The author and publishers wish to express their thanks to the following sources of illustrative material and/or permission to reproduce it.

photo: Donald Cooper / Rex Features: p. 164; © DACS p. 93; photo Ian Dryden/Rex Features: p. 24; Gemäldegalerie Dresden: p. 170; from an issue of *L'Illustration* from 1895: p. 46; photos Marilyn Kingwill / ArenaPAL: pp. 10, 141, 158; photo Andy Lopez / Library of Congress, Washington, DC: p. 21; photos courtesy the National Library of Ireland, Dublin: pp. 27, 34; reproduced courtesy of the Headmaster, Portora Royal School, Enniskillen: p. 28; photo Rex Features: p. 137; Staatliche Kunstsammlungen, Dresden: p. 89; photos © Studio Lipnitzki / Roger-Viollet, courtesy Rex Features: pp. 129, 130, 132, 134; Tate Modern, London (photo © Tate, London 2008): p. 93.